PHILIP PENDLETON COOKE

From the Cyclopaedia of American Biographies, *1900*
The signature is in Cooke's handwriting

PHILIP PENDLETON COOKE

By

John D. Allen

CHAPEL HILL · 1942

The University of North Carolina Press

Copyright, 1942, by
The University of North Carolina Press

Foreword

This study grew out of my dissertation, Philip Pendleton Cooke: A Critical and Biographical Study, done at Vanderbilt University, 1939 (unpublished), in which I assembled all of the available data about one of the least known of those minor American writers who deserve a place in literary history.

The present study was originally planned as a biographical introduction to an edition of Cooke's uncollected poetry and prose. Criticism was to be subordinated to biography; from the writings, themselves, the reader might draw his own conclusions as to the merits of Cooke's work. The project of an edition, however, has been postponed until more settled times; and in consequence this study, published in the hope of stimulating interest in Cooke, has been revised to present more interpretation than was at first thought necessary. But it retains all of the important data in the dissertation, and it remains mostly biography. Problems that would concern only the special student, such as identification of Cooke's unsigned contributions to periodicals or the authorship of unpublished manuscript sketches of his life, are omitted. They are considered at length in the dissertation; and the student will also find there a much fuller documentation than was considered necessary in an account intended for the more general reader.

Scholars who desire to know more about Cooke may find helpful the bibliography of my dissertation, which is printed at the end of this study. It contains all the references cited in the text and footnotes.

Materials for a life of Cooke were widely scattered, and I am indebted to a variety of sources for the information I have employed. For use of special collections in the Duke University Library, the library of Peabody Institute, the Library of Congress, the New York Public Library, the Boston Public Library, the library of Harvard University, and the library of Princeton University, I am greatly indebted. Other libraries whose manuscript collections and periodical files have also been helpful include those of the University of North Carolina, the University of Virginia, the Virginia Historical Society, the Virginia State Historical Society, the Maryland Historical Society, the University of Pennsylvania, the Pennsylvania Historical Society, Columbia University, the American Antiquarian Society, Yale University, and the Hendley Library, Winchester, Virginia. Records in the Martinsburg, Virginia, Court House provided data for the genealogy of Cooke.

Mrs. Archibald B. Bevan of Millwood, Va., and Miss Anne Meade of Baltimore, granddaughters of Cooke, gave invaluable aid by granting free use of manuscript materials, as did Cooke's niece, Miss Mariah P. Duval of Charlottesville, Va., and his nephew, Dr. R. P. Cooke of Lexington. Other relatives who aided are Mrs. Charles Lee of Sea Island, Ga., Mrs. Jennie Winston Hunter of Doswell, Va., and the late Mr. Edward D. Quarles, secretary of the Valentine Museum, Richmond, Va.

I gratefully acknowledge the information given me by Dr. William H. Whiting, Jr., of Hampden-Sydney College, Virginia, and the late J. H. Whitty of Richmond. I am especially indebted to P. W. Turrentine of the University of Arkansas for copies of three letters from Cooke to Nathaniel Beverley Tucker, and to Dr. Edd Winfield Parks of the University of Georgia for having interested me in Cooke—and for his continuing interest in this study.

My debt is greatest to my wife, without whose assistance and encouragement I would have known less about Philip Pendleton Cooke.

JOHN D. ALLEN.

Contents

CHAPTER	PAGE
Foreword	v
I. Early Years	3
II. Princeton	13
III. Poetry and Love	20
IV. Martinsburg, the West, and the Law	38
V. The Vineyard and *Froissart Ballads*	63
VI. Prose Works	87
VII. Last Years	100
Bibliography	106
Index	121

ILLUSTRATIONS

Phil P. Cooke	*Frontispiece*
Manuscript of "Florence Vane"	*facing p.* 30

PHILIP PENDLETON COOKE

CHAPTER I

Early Years

MINDFUL OF THE dignity expected of a Virginia gentleman and poet, Philip Pendleton Cooke wrote down on paper in the early autumn of 1845 such modest account of his life as seemed not improper to render the reading public. Rufus W. Griswold was about to launch another of his popular literary anthologies; Cooke was to be included; and there had been correspondence, mainly through and with his cousin in Baltimore, John Pendleton Kennedy, chief of the Kennedy-Cooke literary clan. Would Cooke send some of his verses to Griswold? And a biography?

Cooke would, and did, though not before Mr. Kennedy had warned him that certain poems must be forwarded at once or lose a place in the new edition of the *Poets and Poetry of America*. Cooke had found himself very much interrupted, he informed Griswold, and that must make his excuse for the shortcomings of the pieces he enclosed. He was sending "Emily—Proem to the Froissart Ballads," which Griswold would perceive had been thoroughly elaborated; he supposed it was too long for Griswold's purpose. Of the smaller pieces "Young Rosalie Lee" was published ten years ago, "and *took* in the South singularly well, considering the flippancies of phraseology and false rhymes &c. that disfigure it—but which I have never ventured to change. I send it to you because it did take." The other enclosures had never been published. He had many other pieces which he had intended to retouch and send, so that

Griswold might have a full budget to select from; "but I 'put it off,' was interrupted, and now must send you what I have without delay."

As for his biography, he might say with Canning's knife-grinder, "I have none." He was born on October 26, 1816, in the town of Martinsburg, Berkeley County, Virginia. His father, John R. Cooke, was and had long been a man of honorable distinction in the bar of the state. His mother, Maria Pendleton, was sister to John Pendleton Kennedy's mother. For himself, he had spent several years at Princeton and, he believed, graduated, although he never distinguished himself or took an honor.

While at Princeton he had contributed several pieces of verse to the *Knickerbocker;* and on his return to Winchester, where his father then resided, "I began (then 18) to write prose and verse for the Messenger, then just started. Before 21 I was a lawyer and married; my wife was Willianne Burwell; I am happy by my fireside at this place on the banks of the Shenandoah, in view, and within a mile, of the Blue Ridge. I go to county towns, at the sessions of courts, and hunt and fish, and make myself as happy with my companions as I can." He had lately spurred himself again into continuous composition and meant "to *finish* books." He had already projected several. "And this is the 'sum and story' of this 'human life' of mine."[1]

This much about himself Cooke thought proper to unfold to Griswold and the public; and if he could make anything out of such material, Cooke would wonder at his skill.

Griswold made the usual sketch for his *Poets and Poetry of America,* to which he added apparently sincere praise of Cooke's talent. Many of Mr. Cooke's pieces were very beau-

---

1. Griswold Collection, Boston Public Library. Letter, Philip Pendleton Cooke to Rufus W. Griswold, dated October 15, 1845. Cooke referred to the *Southern Literary Messenger,* founded in Richmond by T. W. White in August, 1834. The *Knickerbocker Magazine* was established in 1833.

Early Years

tiful, Griswold believed. His "Florence Vane" was one of the most poetical songs that had been written in this country. His longer poems were elaborate, "full of striking thoughts and delicate fancies"; and nearly all of them contained touches of tenderness which showed to what issues his spirit was attuned.[2]

The young poet thus launched by the industrious popularizer of America's literary geniuses, soon to be launched under his own name in a less successful work,[3] had been as fortunate as most Virginians in the matter of ancestry. His mother's family, the Pendletons, had been Tidewater folk since 1674, when Philip Pendleton had come from England to Virginia consigned as an indentured servant to a certain Captain Crask, then living in the parish of South Farnham in Essex County. The family had prospered and multiplied; and Pendleton men had been Revolutionary patriots, judges, statesmen. Pendleton women, marrying Claytons, Barbours, Kennedys, Strothers, Gaineses, Cookes, had produced or were to produce offspring prominent in the culture of Virginia and the Middle States.

Meanwhile one branch of the family had joined that stream of Tidewater stock which, reaching the northern Shenandoah Valley in the seventeen-thirties, was to mingle, though not readily to blend, with the Dutch, Scotch-Irish, and German settlers moving down from the north. From this branch descended Maria Pendleton, mother of Philip Pendleton Cooke.

The Cookes had also come from England, family tradition runs, where, in County Hereford, Cookes were gentry folk and had their coat-of-arms. From an early migrant to New England descended Nathaniel Cooke, a patriotic Philadel-

---

[2]. R. W. Griswold, ed., *Poets and Poetry of America*, pp. 467-470. The poems selected were "Emily," "Life in the Autumn Woods," and "Florence Vane."

[3]. P. P. Cooke, *Froissart Ballads and Other Poems*, published in Philadelphia by Carey and Hart early in 1847. This is the only volume of Cooke's poetry.

phia merchant during the Revolution. Nathaniel was the father of Stephen, physician and patriot, who while a prisoner of war in the Bermudas fell in love with Catherine Esten, daughter of the governor of the islands, John Esten. They were married after the Revolution, and Stephen Cooke settled in Alexandria, Va. Later he acquired a landed estate near Leesburg, in Loudoun County, where he died in 1816, the year of his poet-grandson's birth.

Two of Stephen Cooke's sons—John Esten, the eldest, and Philip St. George, the youngest—became figures of more than local note, the former in medicine and in the ministry, the latter as author of works concerned with military matters and as a brigadier general in the Union forces during the War Between the States. A third, John Rogers Cooke, born in Bermuda in 1788, moved conspicuously for many years on the Virginia legal stage.

Despite the precision of his manners and the elegance of his dress, traits for which he was noted throughout his life, John R. Cooke prospered in the back-country village of Martinsburg, where as a young lawyer he settled about the year 1810. His marriage with Maria Pendleton three years later allied him with leading families of Martinsburg and Berkeley County. His keenness of mind and his great skill as a trial lawyer adequately rewarded his clients and won for him a reputation not confined to Virginia. In addition to a lavish generosity, however, he exhibited a lack of business judgment surprising in one of his legal ability, a weakness which no doubt contributed to the later loss of his fortune.

Cooke moved to Winchester, county seat of Frederick County, in 1828, and then to nearby "Glengary," the dowry of his wife, where he continued to be the prosperous barrister and generous, almost spendthrift, gentleman. Circumstances altered, however, with the panic of 1837, and shortly Cooke

Early Years

was beset with financial cares. Then Glengary burned. He moved in 1839 to nearby Charlestown, and, in March of 1840, to Richmond, where for the rest of his life he struggled to free himself of debt. There, almost five years after the death of his wife, he died in December, 1854.[4]

Debts were to plague Philip Pendleton Cooke, too, during most of the years of his manhood, with no great success at the bar such as the father had achieved to lessen the sting of poverty, and no dreamed-of career as a statesman such as, had he dreamed of it, the father might easily have achieved. In the meantime, there was a boyhood to be spent.

So far as the scanty family records reveal, it was not an unhappy boyhood. The first mention of Philip Pendleton Cooke occurs in a letter from Catherine Esten to her lawyer-son. The times were bad; a tenant had been remiss in payment of rent for certain land; there were other irksome matters about which she needed advice. Maria, a paragraph added, might count on a visit in October at the meeting of the Presbytery in Martinsburg. "My darling Ann will, by that time, be so improved that it will be quite a treat to look at her beloved countenance. The dear little Philip too will be old enough to walk." She anticipated much pleasure from this visit.[5]

It is certain that, in time, Philip learned to walk; but on this, as on other personal matters of his childhood and youth,

4. Of Cooke's thirteen children, only four survived him. Two daughters, Mary Pendleton and Sarah Dandridge, married and settled in Richmond. John Esten, unmarried until after the Civil War, during which he gathered experiences for his once widely read war novels, had in the meantime studied law in Richmond and begun his career as an author. A younger son, Edward St. George, talented with both pen and artist's pencil, died in early manhood in 1858. Eight other children died in infancy or youth. The eldest son, the subject of this study, died of pneumonia in 1850, just as he had achieved literary maturity and recognition.

5. Miss Mariah Pendleton Duval, Charlottesville, Virginia. Letter from Catherine Esten Cooke to John R. Cooke, dated March 22, 1817. "My darling Ann" was the first of the thirteen children of John R. Cooke.

even family tradition is almost wholly silent. Perhaps he played with his cousin Philip Pendleton Kennedy, who, however, when he came to write Philip's biography, knew and had learned little that might not be said of most boys. That Philip did play with, and was a schoolmate of, another cousin, the artist David H. Strother, the Kennedy cousin recorded. But of those years Strother, too, remembered little "except that Philip was a handsome boy, with large brown eyes, and dark curling hair, sprightly and amiable.—For the rest he was like other boys—and I never heard that he gave any peculiar promise for the future."[6]

Possibly the environment of Martinsburg was hardly one to evoke in a youth of Philip's temperament early signs of aesthetic promise. True, since 1812 there had been a Martinsburg Academy, where among other subjects one might study Latin and Greek; and doubtless in Philip's time the curriculum offered all that a healthy boy would care to absorb.[7] But there is no evidence, beyond Strother's remark, that Philip attended the academy, nor anything to suggest that, had he done so, it would have kindled poetic fire.

The town of Martinsburg, itself, although the center and county seat of prosperous Berkeley, remained a semi-frontier settlement. Less than a century earlier all had been wilder-

---

[6] From an unpublished manuscript memoir of Cooke by his cousin Philip Pendleton Kennedy, in the possession of Cooke's granddaughter, Mrs. Archibald B. Bevan, of Millwood, Va. The memoir, mostly rhetoric, contains few details of biographical or critical value. Strother, who gained much fame for his illustrations in Union periodicals during the War Between the States, is perhaps better known under his nom de plume, "Porte Crayon."

[7] An announcement of the winter session in the *Martinsburg Gazette* for Sept. 10, 1840, lists the following subjects as taught: reading, writing, arithmetic, geography, grammar, history, composition, elocution, Latin, Greek, mental and natural philosophy, chemistry, French, and the higher branches of mathematics. Thorough instruction in these subjects was promised, and "the discipline of the school will be mild, but effective; and no pains spared to secure the greatest amount of study, and a correct, gentlemanly deportment." Philip C. Pendleton and other Cooke relatives were named as trustees.

ness, part of the hardly known region separated by the barrier of the Blue Ridge from populated Virginia. Then, in 1732, had come "the restless Johannes Joosten Hite with his twenty families, and they with horses and wagons, with milch cattle and flocks, and above all with a determination to remain all their days in this Valley of the Shenando."[8]

Scotch-Irish and German settlers followed the Dutch; and after Lord Fairfax had built his hunting lodge, Greenway Court, at White Post in 1748, began the wave of immigration from middle and Tidewater Virginia—"sons of the landed Gentry—true Cavalier stock." Now "The Valley was rapidly filling with eager settlers. Tobacco, corn and wheat were grown upon the early plantations. The spinning wheel whirred. The flocks and herds toiled up the slopes of Blue Ridge, eastward moving, to Alexandria, to Dumfries and Fredericksburg, where the ships lay. Clarke (and with Clarke the whole region) had entered into the world's commerce." And soon "the Red Men vanished into the west, forever, as the pioneers thronged down from Packhorse Ford on the north, from the Blue Ridge on the east."[9]

These two distinct streams of migrants, not even yet wholly fused in their descendants, doubtless determined the atmosphere of the two towns where was spent Cooke's youth: Martinsburg, settled mainly by Dutch, Scotch-Irish, and Germans; and Winchester, dominated by Tidewater scions who, before and after the Revolution, had acquired large grants of land in the surrounding countryside. Effects of the two environments may be traced in Cooke's writings. For example, his first short novel, *John Carper, the Hunter of Lost River*, reflects both in its characters and in its setting the homespun society of the Martinsburg area during the Revolution; it may well have grown out of such a tale as a

---

8. Arthur Bowie Chrisman, "A History of Clarke County," Everard Kidder Meade, ed., *Clarke County, 1836-1936*, p. 5.

9. *Ibid.*, pp. 5, 8. Clarke County was formed from Berkeley in 1836.

smart youngster might still have heard from some ancient veteran in the Martinsburg of 1825. Part of Cooke's poem, "The Mountains," suggests the same background. On the other hand, *The Two Country Houses* obviously reflects—though perhaps with a romantic mirror—Winchester and the gentry of Frederick County.

The extent to which Cooke was later attracted by the Frederick gentry and its diversions is suggested by a letter written some years before his death to Griswold. It had occurred to him to turn his passion for hunting, and his "'crowding experiences' (gathered in fifteen or sixteen years of life in the merriest Virginia Society) of hunting, fishing, country races, character and want of character, woods, mountains, fields and water," into a rambling book.[10] The design was never carried out, although the posthumously published essay-anecdote "The Turkey-hunter in the Closet" may well have been intended as a chapter for such a book.

In the meantime the Cookes had moved, in 1828, to Winchester and the house on Ambler's Hill, where until his entrance at Princeton University Cooke was to live. Of his years in Winchester no record in his own hand remains. Perhaps Aunt Catherine heard his lessons, a service she was to perform for John Esten; perhaps, like John Esten later, he played with tops, or listened to old tales from the lips of Grandmother Esten—a quiet, deeply religious-looking old lady, as the younger grandson remembered her, calmly knitting. Perhaps on hunting jaunts with his older cousin, Philip Pendleton Kennedy, then in attendance at the law school of the noted Judge Henry St. George Tucker in

---

10. [John Esten Cooke] "Recollections of Philip Pendleton Cooke," *Southern Literary Messenger*, XXVI (June, 1858), 421. Unsigned. Identity of the author is established in the present writer's dissertation. Manuscript of the article is in the possession of Dr. R. P. Cooke.

Early Years

Winchester, he learned that skill with the rifle for which he was afterward to become, among the gentry of the Valley, as renowned as for his poetry. And perhaps he scribbled verses to his cousin Mary Evelina Hunter Dandridge, later to be celebrated in the poem "Florence Vane." That before he entered Princeton he had already begun to write is indicated by his cousin David K. Strother.

"I never heard of Philip's showing any talent for versification," Strother informed Pendleton Kennedy, "until he was about fourteen or fifteen." About that time he had acquired "a boy's reputation among friends and relations," and Strother sent him a copy from a French caricature of a poet—"represented, in a sublime reverie, biting the end of his quill and with a quire of blank paper before him," beneath which Strother had written a quotation from Shakespeare. The letter continued:

"The receipt of the caricature was acknowledged by a good-humored message, and a present of some books. A year or more later I received a letter from him requesting me to make a sketch illustrating some lines of poetry, which he said he had taken from some old volume, and which struck me at the time as very fine. They referred to a class of subjects of which he was always an admirer—stories of feudal romance. I have forgotten the lines, but remember the drawing, which was, a castle moss-grown and dilapidated, with a hound whining at the gate, and a neglected steed looking wistfully through the bars of the portcullis. I was not pleased with the execution of the drawing, and did not send it to him. Some months afterwards, however, he visited me, and seeing the piece on the table among others, he recognized it, and inquired if that were not the drawing I had made for him, and took it, saying that it expressed his idea fully and beautifully. I told him playfully, that I supposed he meant the idea he got from the old volume; at which he laughingly acknowledged the authorship of the lines."[11]

Cooke attended the academy in Winchester,[12] but of what he studied there he nowhere speaks. In 1831, at the age of fifteen, he entered Princeton.

11. Kennedy Memoir.
12. A note in his file among the Princeton University alumni records reads: "Prepared for P. U. at Mr. Bruce's academy, Winchester, Va." No source for the information is indicated. The only relevant mention of a Mr. Bruce occurs in J. E. Norris, *History of the Lower Shenandoah Valley*, p. 177. Discussing the Winchester newspapers, Norris notes: "E. C. Bruce published the *Virginian* for several years prior to" the Civil War. The same paragraph indicates one great difficulty encountered in the effort to collect Cooke's early poetry, much of which was published in Winchester newspapers. Bruce sold the *Virginian* "to J. J. Palmer, who moved the office up the valley in 1862, where it was destroyed. George E. Senseny published the *Republican* for a number of years before the war, and sold to Nathaniel B. Meade, who ran the paper until Gen. Banks came into the Valley, in the spring of 1862, when the plant was destroyed by the soldiers." No files of these papers for the early years have, it would seem, survived.

CHAPTER II

Princeton

To A SERIOUS-MINDED youth of fifteen, well read for his age and already a scribbler of verses, the village of Princeton probably offered in the early eighteen-thirties few attractions not equaled in Winchester or Martinsburg. Except, of course, the college and its library—principally the library. Eight thousand volumes it contained, the Princeton authorities boasted; and among them must have been many of which even a well-read boy would not have heard. Among the courses of instruction, too, heavily loaded with mathematics and the classics, must have been some that would appeal strongly to a poetic mind; for example, Homer's *Iliad,* which he might study in the summer session of the sophomore year, or belles-lettres and Greek tragedy, which were required in his senior year. And at the option of the student, French, Spanish, German, or Italian—valuable, they could be, to a prospective poet—might be taken without extra charge.[1]

Of what Cooke actually did during and with his years at Princeton, the few surviving records reveal little. The very sketchy manuscript volume, Minutes of the Faculty,[2] records the fact that on May 17, 1832, Cooke was examined and admitted to the sophomore class. Some weeks later he addressed to his father the only letter that remains from his

---

1. For a full statement of the curriculum and other interesting details see the pamphlet *Princeton: Courses of Instruction (1839-40),* in the Princeton University library.
2. In the Princeton library.

youth and early manhood, one of the few letters, in fact, that have survived from the years prior to 1840.

This was the fourth time, he complained, that he had written home, and not one word had he received in return. He could not account for it except by supposing that "your letters may have miscarried. Phil P—— has received 2 letters and Stephen & Ed P—— each one (from home)."[3] From the boys he had learned that his family were all well, "and that Aunt D—— was in Winchester," which greatly relieved his fears.[4]

They were all very comfortably situated there at Princeton. His fellow students were, most of them, fine, openhearted fellows. He knew of but one or two among the number who were really dissipated. Now that he had become acquainted with all around him, his situation had lost most of that irksomeness which he had felt upon leaving a land where nearly all were his acquaintances and friends for a land of strangers. It was now about half after six (morning). He had been up ever since five and had attended both prayers and recitations.

His father had told him, he believed, that about the middle of the summer he might come to Princeton. Nothing would delight more than to see him "among us," which, considering the rapidity with which one was able to travel at the present day, would be no arduous task and would detain him a very short time from his business at home.

He had written thus far when the breakfast horn blew, after which, on going to the post office, he had found "a letter from Ma." It had been sixteen days, it seemed, in coming. He was certain some one had written. The tutor

3. Philip Pendleton, Jr., Stephen Dandridge, and Edmund Pendleton, all three of whom were nephews of Cooke's mother.
4. The reason for his relief is obscure, though "Aunt D——" was the mother of Mary Evelina Hunter Dandridge, a relationship which, in view of Cooke's fondness for his cousin, may help to explain his solicitude.

would be around in a moment or two and he must necessarily close. His love was to be given "to Ma and all. Tell Sister A—— that she must answer my letters—as soon as she can do so conveniently. I hope you will be here this summer but for the present—adieu—." A postscript requested, "Write to me, and let me know particularly how the house comes on."[5]

The few brief references to Cooke in the Minutes of the Faculty confirm the tradition that he was both a sensitive, high-spirited youth and, in the judgment of the Princeton faculty, hardly a luminary of the first magnitude in the realm of formal scholarship. During the winter session of his junior year he was in Section IV of a class which had four sections. For the winter session of his senior year he averaged, with two others, seventy-four, attaining thereby the rank of eighteenth in a class of thirty-four. And less than a month before he was to receive his degree, he and a fellow-student were suspended from the college "for a mutual personal assault upon each other," Cooke indefinitely, his fellow for a period of two weeks.[6]

No inkling of the origin of the altercation eluded the restraints of academic decorum, which was satisfied with the baldest statement of fact. There is no reason, however, to suppose that such incidents were rarer then than now, or more important, even though by college faculties they were then deemed worthy of grave action. At any rate, Cooke did not long remain suspended. Three days after the

5. From the original in the possession of Miss Mariah P. Duval, Charlottesville, Virginia. Dated "Princeton/June 5th/32 (Tuesday morning)." The house to which Cooke alluded was Glengary, the country estate near Winchester to which the Cookes moved in 1833.
6. Minutes of the Faculty. Entry dated July 17, 1834. About the fellow-student, a sophomore named Charles S. Hammond, practically no relevant information is contained in his file among the alumni records. The Faculty Minutes note that, a year after his altercation with Cooke, he and another student "were suspended from College, for going to the tavern without permission." (Entry for July 21, 1835).

regular senior examinations this entry appeared in the Minutes: "Mr. Philip P. Cooke, who was suspended from the College on the 17th ult., was admitted to examination:—and the Faculty, having examined him, resolved to recommend him, with the other members of the class, to the Board of Trustees for the first Degree in the Arts."[7]

A quick temper is said to have had a part in another incident of Cooke's undergraduate days, described half a century later in correspondence from Shepherdstown in a Richmond, Virginia, newspaper. "I had a night and part of a day," writes the anonymous roving correspondent, "with Hon. Alexander R. Boteler. . . . He drew for me a rough sketch of his room-mate, Philip Pendleton Cooke. . . . 'Florence Vane' was written in his room. Whenever he wanted to write Cooke dashed everything off the table and one day he dashed on the floor a new suit of Boteler's clothes. In return, Boteler threw out of the window a book which 'Florence Vane' (Mrs. R. M. T. Hunter) had given to the young poet. Instantly there was a fight, but that served to make them better friends than before."[8]

Such stories as the foregoing suggest that despite his reserve and his romantic temperament, Cooke was a sufficiently normal youth, on pleasant enough terms with some, if not all, of his associates. By his fellows in the American Whig Society, composed of students whose families, like his, were foes to Andrew Jackson, he apparently was held in high regard. A resolution of the society, passed some weeks after Cooke's death, referred to his "numerous friends and admirers" and spoke of his "brilliant poetical genius" which had reflected high honor on the institution.[9]

7. Entry for August 13, 1834.
8. *The State*, Richmond, Virginia, Wednesday, April 27, 1881. Boteler's memory probably was in error. Evidence indicates that "Florence Vane" was written in 1839.
9. Reprinted in the *Southern Literary Messenger*, XVI (March, 1850), 192.

Yet he seems to have had few close friends and to have been influenced in his attitudes and his career no more by them than by his instructors. Benjamin H. Brewster, a classmate, remembered him as "remarkable for his pride"; he impressed one as a "stately and dignified youth, who kept himself apart from his fellow-collegians."[10] And John S. Hart, a young instructor in ancient languages during Cooke's years at Princeton, also had "a very vivid recollection" of his character: "proud, resolute, but very sweet-tempered, and remarkable for his dignity and personal beauty. His head was really noble, his eyes dark, his hair curling chestnut, and his person erect and vigorous." The adjectives are not, it is true, original with the instructor. John Esten Cooke supplied them many years later in a sketch of "my brother, of whom you so kindly inquire," published by Hart in a manual of American literature. But fraternal affection, Hart believed, had in its choice of descriptives "barely done justice to one of nature's noblest gentlemen."[11]

Of the academic values offered by the Princeton of his youth, Cooke acquired more than his academic standing would suggest. The prose essays of his mature years, though not burdened with classical allusions, grew out of a mind well grounded in the classics of Greco-Roman culture; and their style exhibits classic qualities of precision, moderation, and restraint. That he had at least a reading knowledge of French, German, and Italian is clear from examination of his personal letters and his poetry and prose. The chief values Cooke obtained from Princeton, however, and those most observable in his later work were found not in the classroom but in the library—"in studies," Philip Pendle-

 10. "Philip Pendleton Cooke," *Illustrated Monthly Courier*, I, No. 4 (October 2, 1848). Unsigned.
 11. John S. Hart, *A Manual of American Literature*, p. 483. Hart, a graduate of Princeton in 1830, served until 1836 as an instructor.

ton Kennedy remembered, "out of the line of the usual college learning—history, romance, poetry—general literature."[12] He paid more attention to "Belles Lettres, poetry and the departments of elegant learning generally," agreed John Esten Cooke, "than to the dryer, but more important, studies of the Collegiate course." His knowledge of mathematics, philosophy, and languages was appreciative and respectable, "but by no means profound or critical. His attainments were, nearly all, in the direction of polite literature—and were striking and unusual. Wandering at large in the libraries of the College, he seems to have emulated the habits of the bee—to have sought for the sweets of letters, in the 'flowery parterres' of Spenser, Chaucer (always favourites with him) and the elder poets of the language, to whom his devotion continued earnest and unchanging throughout life."[13]

It would be an error, however, to suppose that Cooke—at any rate, the mature Cooke—was indifferent to science or that he knew nothing of the literature of his own day. To his father's home came *The Edinburgh Review* and most of the other leading British periodicals. These would have given him, from boyhood, some acquaintance with contemporary literary figures. One of his critical essays, "Living Novelists," shows intimate knowledge of the works of Bulwer, Dumas, G. P. R. James, D'Israeli, Scott, and Cooper; and other essays and letters, extending the list of prose authors, evidence familiarity with contemporary poetry of England and America.

The letters also evidence Cooke's respect for science. "The exact sciences," he believed, "and history (read with an intelligence that groups facts and puts them away in the Mind) and the best poetry of the best Poets, afford matter enough for any youth no matter how he may devour books,

12, Kennedy Memoir.   13. "Recollections," p. 420.

and should constitute the great bulk of his study until he enters upon professional reading."[14]

Such, in his maturity, was Cooke's advice for his younger brothers. It suggests that, despite his fondness at Princeton for the remote in time and space, he had laid there the foundations of a well-rounded education.

14. Letter, Philip Pendleton Cooke to John R. Cooke, dated October 13, 1843. In the possession of Miss Duval.

CHAPTER III

Poetry and Love

WHEN IN THE summer of 1834 Cooke left Princeton for Winchester, he probably felt little enthusiasm for the task that lay ahead. That task was to gain working knowledge of the law. To the mind, the importance of mastering Blackstone and Lord Coke would appeal with sufficient force. Cooke's father had gained esteem and opulence through the law, and might have gained high public position had he desired that mark of his fellows' regard. Before his father's generation, two generations of ambitious young Virginians had found the law the surest pathway to honor, place, and power. Of Cooke's own generation, among his kinsmen and among his classmates at Princeton, many were destined for the same path—almost all, traditionally, whose futures were not patterned by the inheritance of plantation estates.

There was not, in fact, for a well-born young man moved by the spirit of ambition, much choice beyond Blackstone and Coke. True, one might choose the military profession, in which Uncle Philip St. George was beginning to make a name. And there was the profession of medicine, in which Uncle John Esten had already made a name; and theology, in which he was about to make another. Had Cooke's homecoming been in Boston or Philadelphia or New York, or even in Baltimore, instead of Glengary on the banks of the Opequon near Winchester, Virginia, he might have gone into business, as, it was said, his great-grandfather

Nathaniel had shrewdly done. Or he might, without much detraction from his standing as a gentleman, have frankly become an author—like Irving or Bryant or Cooper—and have taken money without scruple for what his pen produced. But Glengary offered no highway to commerce or banking, and scarcely a trail even to literature. About all Cooke could descry on the literary horizon was the chance of a reputation like that of, for example, Richard Henry Wilde, whose poetry, the product of a gentleman-lawyer's leisure, was being reprinted in the *Messenger*.

Besides, had not his father urged that he prepare himself for the law? And apart from the question of filial duty, certainly with Philip Pendleton Cooke a weighty question, was not John R. Cooke a man whose judgment was not to be lightly brushed aside?

Considerations such as these, particularly the latter, would have appealed to Cooke's mind with peculiar weight. Nor is there any evidence that he deliberately rebelled against them. Dutifully he submitted to read and remember enough law for admission to the bar, which, as he afterwards informed Rufus Griswold, he had achieved before he was twenty-one. Until the burning of Glengary and the breakup of his father's family, he may have been of some assistance to the father in a practice which then extended over the counties of Frederick, Berkeley, Jefferson, and Clarke. In his later years he repeatedly turned to the law as a possible means of assuring comfort for his own family. But he knew in those later years that he detested the law; and from the beginning his heart was not in it.

For some months after Cooke's homecoming, literature seems to have had little competition from Blackstone. During the Princeton years Cooke had occasionally written poems, three of which—"Song of the Sioux Lovers," "The Consumptive," and "Dhu Nowas"—appeared in the *Knick-*

erbocker Magazine. John Esten Cooke mentions, in addition to these three, "Count Herman" and "The Moss Troopers," "these all appearing in the Knickerbocker and Winchester papers, where also were published Goluon, Isabel, Kemp, the Glider."[1] Elsewhere he names, as composed during the same period, "The Season of Youth," "The Dream," and "Napoleon in Egypt"[2]—a total of twelve published poems, if the memory of the younger brother is to be trusted. Doubtless there were other efforts which Cooke did not consider worthy to submit to publishers.

The easy freedom of peaceful, happy Glengary encouraged for a time the literary experimentation that had begun at Princeton. Two of Cooke's new poems appeared in the *Southern Literary Messenger* for January, 1835; another in the March number, one in the April. Also in the April number was published the first installment of the essay "English Poetry," continued in the number for June. The volume of this published work is not great, but it is probably only a small part of all Cooke actually wrote during the period. Ten years later he spoke in a letter to his father of "six months of continuous composition, such as that at Glengary in my nineteenth year."[3] Since his pen was a fluent one, and since little else from the period survives, many of his compositions, still in manuscript form, must have perished in the burning of Glengary in 1839, when everything of value was destroyed.

If the quality of the manuscripts destroyed was no higher than that of the published work, it must be conceded that literature suffered no heavy loss. Cooke's poetic talent matured slowly. In his early productions, both poetry and

1. Griswold Collection. Letter, John Esten Cooke to Rufus W. Griswold, June 6, 1851. A complete list of Cooke's known extant poems is given in the Appendix.
2. Manuscript diary of John Esten Cooke, in the possession of his son, Dr. R. P. Cooke, Lexington, Va.
3. Cooke Collection, Duke University. Dated July 6, 1844.

Poetry and Love

prose, he was rarely himself; he was almost always, rather, the reflector of what he had read in his favorite authors or in the periodical literature of the day. Only in "Rosalie Lee" and, very occasionally, in a line or so in other verses is there promise of the future poet. As records of his youth, these immaturities have a certain value, as do the poems of the Princeton years; and for an author in embryo they were useful exercises. But if the estimate of Cooke as a poet were to rest solely on what he had published before the close of his nineteenth year, there would be slight excuse for disturbing the oblivion into which his name has fallen.

Cooke's own estimate of the worth of his youthful productions and his judgment as to the possibilities of a career in literature are expressed in two letters to Nathaniel Beverley Tucker, composed late in 1835. Tucker, who recently had been made professor of law at William and Mary College, had formed connections with the *Messenger;* and in its infancy he was able to render much assistance to the publisher and nominal editor, T. W. White, through the reading of manuscripts and in the offering of critical advice. For some motive, perhaps because he recognized the genuine talent beneath the artificialities and crudities of youth, Tucker wrote to Cooke during the summer of 1835. Unfortunately, neither this nor any other of his letters to the younger man seems to have been preserved. Cooke's reply, however, makes it obvious that at least in part Tucker's object was to offer an encouragement which the recipient was in no present mood to accept:

"You were kind enough in your letter of some months ago to half invite a correspondence. I need hardly assure you that this will give me much pleasure. Many a pleasant matter comes from an unpleasant source, and I shall thank the unlucky beginning of our imperfect acquaintance if you write to me again and often.

"The stuff that you criticised to White and, through him, to me, certainly deserved harsh treatment. I had however some excuse for thinking it worth publishing:—my father (only a tolerable judge of Poetry) praised it highly—so did other friends, at the time in the house, at the request of one of whom the verses were written—*hurriedly*. I say 'hurriedly' for they and some half dozen more rejected stanzas were written at a single sitting—perhaps in two hours.

"My standard of poetic excellence is very high, and I rarely fail to see, after the excitement of composition has passed away, the want of merit in my pieces. None of them have *any* merit, me judice, except a short piece which you may have seen—'Rosalie Lee.' This I haven't seen since it was published, and only remember as a rather pretty extravaganza. However, if I thought them all as they should be, I would *now* care nothing for criticism, as I have given up Poetry and verse making. Parnassus—so far as crops of worldly produce—dollars—are concerned is as barren as a worn-out tobacco field. Besides a Poet's reputation, even if he succeeds to the top of his wishes, is of little or no avail—as it comes too late. We can warm to no poetry that hasn't a mistress coupled with our thought of the Poet:—while he lives there is too much flesh and blood reality about our thought of him—too little mistiness. Byron was popular as a Poet because the humbug mystery of his bearing, and the eccentricity of his fortunes, were not discovered to be the one a humbug and the other a most *unromantic* eccentricity. Other writers have gained present reputation by their poetical works from the peculiarity of the works themselves; they have been such as to enable one to form no idea whatever of the author—to keep him in a mysterious darkness—the mysterious invisibility of the nightingale whose song we listen to.

"But this is all nonsense I fear, or at any rate useless—

perspicua vera non probanda sunt. Pardon the Latin—I am just now fresh from Lord Coke, and 'smell of the shop.'

"I haven't your letter by me, but I remember that you speak of the deep interest you take in the Messenger. I sincerely trust that your interest will be active. The only monthly magazine of the South ought hardly to depend for support upon the feeble efforts of boys. *I am just nineteen* and have reason to believe myself older than a majority of Mr. White's contributors.

"In an article of my own—English Poetry, chap. II.—published during your absence, Mr. White made so many typographical errors that I wrote to him severely. If you read the article please make allowances for these errors.

"My father begs to be presented to you. I must conclude. Let me assure you, my dear Sir, that your criticism *was* 'taken in good part' and believe me ever Yours truly P. P. Cooke."[4]

Tucker's answer to the foregoing evidently counseled against Cooke's decision to give up poetry for Lord Coke. But the advice was for the moment unavailing. Tucker's letter had been mislaid, Cooke replied in December, 1835, but he had read it more than once and recalled its contents. He had noted the main point in Tucker's counsel, that it would be worth while for him—"author of some few tame verses and of 'a compilation which any one might compile' "[5]—to come before the public a candidate for reputa-

---

[4]. From P. W. Turrentine's copy of the original in the Coleman Manuscript Collection, Tucker House, Williamsburg, Va. Letter dated October 25, 1835. Abbreviations in the original have been spelled out, and punctuation has been somewhat altered to conform with present usage. Other letters of Cooke have been similarly changed.

[5]. Here, as in other passages in the letter, Cooke evidently quotes phrases from Tucker's previous letters, from Tucker's novel, *George Balcombe*, or from his criticism to White, which in some way may have come to Cooke's notice. The allusion is to the essay "English Poetry," which, however, is more than a mere compilation.

tion and pay as an author. He had noted, too, the ways and means by which Tucker had suggested success would be attained. They were certainly well pointed out, and the advice was wise and sound. If ever he became a candidate for reputation and pay as an author, he would certainly follow it:

"But, my dear Sir, all things have a hindrance. The 'student of 19' may not be 'clogged by the habits which fit the man of fifty for the pursuit of an intricate profession and unfit him for every thing else':—he may not have 'mouths to feed—a family to chain him down to the one path,' but he may have, and oftenest *has,* other and serious hindrances. Mindful of the value of your own time, I will enter at once 'into the middle of things.'

"The profession (Law) for which I am preparing myself with some little enthusiasm, and which I have been taught by my Father to look upon as a road to distinction and wealth, is so far removed from 'pleasant poesies' that it is impossible to reconcile them. One or the other must be given up. You think, and say, that at 19 so much life is before one that the pursuit of 'light letters' may be begun and failed in, and still allow a sufficiency of after time for more arduous and *certain* pursuits. (I have made a bungling sentence of that—I am too unwell to write clearly. It conveys my meaning.) I have to answer that, altho 'there may be *time* enough after failure,' yet the mind is little fitted, depressed as it must be by failure, frittered away as it must be by frivolous pursuit, cowed, diseased, dreamy, and timid, as it can't help being—for beginning *de novo* a dull and difficult profession. This is a general objection. I have objections arising from my own peculiar situation. A large mass of business awaits me. The sooner I am prepared to receive it the better. I have other spurs to a close and immediate study of the Law. These are of a nature too sacred to be written. You will perhaps think them 'housed in the heart'—that, loved and loving, I pant for the hour when a long season of 'painful love, of sworn allegiance,' shall be rewarded by else than the pleasant meeting—the stolen kiss—the hurried word, of all which, as the author of 'Romance of real life' &c., you must know very well. Think these thing if you choose.

"As a lawyer reputation and fortune await me. I say this from no idle vanity. I have power of study—close study —and fluency of speech. These with very *little* brain would ensure success. Besides, my Father's business is so extensive that I will be launched by means of it into practice *at once*. He has promised me much of it.

"As an author (*of poetry*) a painful fear of the world's censure—a restless ache of mind—a morbid yearning after the high place among men—(painful, all painful, during their unquiet life, and terrible when failure follows them) await me. I would not live that shrinking and sensitive and cowering existence for—*success*. And what chance would there be of this. Even Wn. Irving was 'wretchedly poor for years'—a type of temporary failure *in prose*. But look at our Poets. Bryant (the master of them all) has sheltered himself from starvation behind the columns of a political newspaper. [Illegible] have no room for eminence, but one and all have found no means of support in 'printing their inspiration.'

"If in the course of time I find it possible to loosen some of the strings binding me to my profession I will imitate my cousin J. P. Kennedy and become a novelist. I will dress what Poetry of thought I may possess, in prose—the dress will make it sell—and *the sale of a book and the reputation of its author certainly go together.* It is for this reason that in speaking of 'failure' I have spoken of 'want of pay.'

One is the sign of the other. But authorship will be a matter of secondary consideration.

"That I am compelled by circumstances (some of them peculiar) to act not in accordance with your kind counsel, does not hinder me from valuing it highly, or from thanking you for interest taken by a stranger, in my welfare. That word *stranger* sounds harshly upon my ear when applied to a 'Tucker.' Living in the same town with your brother—his sons my school-mates—the name has become familiar to my ear. But I must end. Adieu.—P. P. Cooke."[6]

There need be no doubt that in the expression of his resolve to give up poetry and verse-making, Cooke was wholly sincere. But the *Messenger* for January, 1836, contained the rather long poem "Lady Leonore and Her Lover," in addition to the third chapter of "English Poetry"; and other contributions were published in the April, May, and August numbers. Then, indeed, his poetic labors practically ceased. Between August, 1836, and September, 1840, nothing that can be identified beyond doubt as Cooke's appeared in the pages of the *Messenger,* and only two or three casual exercises appeared elsewhere.

For this period of almost complete literary idleness, doubtless the law was to some degree responsible. But not wholly. With Cooke's inactivity and, later, perhaps with his re-awakened interest in poetry, seems to have been correlated at least as closely as the law the course of his relations with his cousin, Mary Evelina Dandridge.

When the attachment between the two first began—for that it was mutual there seems little doubt—it would be idle to speculate. Throughout the years of childhood and youth there had been ample opportunity for meetings. The Dandridges lived at the "Bower," near Charlestown in Jefferson

---

6. From P. W. Turrentine's copy of the original in the Coleman Manuscript Collection. Letter dated December 23, 1835.

Poetry and Love

County, where on October 2, 1817, Mary Evelina was born; and during both Cooke's youth at Martinsburg, sixteen miles away, and his years at Winchester, not much farther, there would have been frequent visits to the Bower, and frequent visits from the family there to Pendleton, Tucker, and Cooke kin. Mary Evelina's mother, Sarah Pendleton, had married Adam Stephen Dandridge, whose grandfather, Captain Alexander Spotswood, had won during the Revolution the hand of General Adam Stephen's only daughter, Ann. And so it came about that Mary Evelina was related to most of the gentry families in the Lower Shenandoah, especially since her great-grandmother, by marrying a second husband, had related her to the Hunters and to the Tuckers. For Ann Evelina Hunter, daughter of Ann Stephen and Moses Hunter, was the wife of Judge Henry St. George Tucker, of Winchester, and hence the sister-in-law of Beverley Tucker, Cooke's correspondent.

How much Mary Evelina Dandridge and Philip Pendleton Cooke were concerned with tables of genealogy must remain among the many minor aspects of their romance upon which records shed no light. What appears certain is that "at about the age of sixteen," as the cautiously verbose and vague Kennedy memoir puts it, "Philip found himself one morning, or night, desperately enamored of a very captivating young lady of his own kindred—she was tall, and she was blythe, and she was debonair, as his own verses describe her, and also she was lovable; for she had by nature that pitying eye, which aided by beauty, is the bow and spear of a maiden ever victorious over the hearts of the youth around her." And, Kennedy continues, Philip fell early in the action, "to all seeming mortally wounded." But nothing ever came of it, for:

"The young gentleman goes off to college, just at the time the elate and joyous maiden—aspirant all of the future—

Hope smiling its enchantments before her, and waving her golden hair, (according to the fine line of Campbell)—just at the time the maiden commences the development of herself to the world of *mankind* around her; and as a matter of course—(to say nothing of the lady's) no young gentleman's sentiment possesses at that age the hardy qualities that are essential to endurance; and so what between change of air and new associations—the facility of youth—its general aptitude to be on with the new love, before it is sure of being off with the old; and beside these, the almost certainty there is that a handsome young girl, well dowered, will be pursued, and wooed, and won by maturer men ... so it happened that Cooke's early passion expired in the natural course of things; and he was left, what is the gain of a man in after years—desperately hard as he takes it for a while at the time—a little romance of love, fixed ever after in his soul, that is always a delicious paradise of thought and sentiment, into which his imagination will lead him, ever and again, at intervals, as he follows out the somewhat arid, weary, flat, stale and unprofitable, dusty, and sometimes somewhat miry paths of real life."

The conduct of Cooke's unsuccessful courtship was colored by a gravity and a romantic imagination slightly quixotic for a youth of nineteen in the year 1835. A suggestion of his attitude peeps through the sober summary of his career written almost four decades later by John Esten: "His youth was impulsive and heyday—he would and did gallop twenty miles to throw a bouquet into the window of his cousin 'Florence Vane.' "[7] Other suggestions are scattered in the early pages of the Kennedy memoir. Cooke possessed, Kennedy recalled, a horse descended on the one side from a horse that could just run fast enough to be beaten on all occasions, named the Bald Eagle; and on the other from

---

[7]. John S. Hart, *A Manual of American Literature*, p. 485.

> I loved thee long and dearly,
>   Florence Vane;
> My life's bright dream and early,
>   Hath come again,
> I renew, in my fond vision,
>   My heart's dear pain,
> My hope, and thy derision
>   Florence Vane.
>
> The ruin lone and hoary,
>   The ruin old
> Where thou did'st hark my story,
>   At even told,—
> That spot—the hues Elysian
>   Of sky and plain—
> I treasure in my vision,
>   Florence Vane.
>
>   Philip Pendleton Cooke

From the Illustrated Library of Favorite Song, *1873*

Manuscript of the first two stanzas of "Florence Vane," written in 1839

some of "the Timorlean stock," which had a certain quality of devilish sulkiness very apt to make them lose a race by bolting. The trappings of this charge were all of black, bloody black, bridle and martingale, saddle and housings; and Philip, himself, Kennedy remembered as dressed in black, even to a black silk cap, which he sometimes wore when he sallied forth, tired of his ruminations, to take his pleasure for a few days throughout the border side.

Cooke was in the habit, continued Kennedy, of mounting Reindeer at night, when the stars shone bright and clear, "and riding some 20 miles across the country—over bank, bush and scaur, adown the wild dells, and through the fords of the lovely stream, to the home of the maiden fair, whom he so worshipped in his young romantic affection." But, as Kennedy has already related, nothing more than poetry came of Cooke's gallantry. Mary Evelina Hunter Dandridge married, in October, 1836, Robert M. T. Hunter, then at the outset of a distinguished career as a Virginia lawyer and statesman.

Despite his distaste for the law and his ill success as a lover, life within the circle of the family at Glengary was in the main happy for Philip Pendleton Cooke. In several letters to his father, a decade later, he speaks with regret of certain aspects of his youthful conduct. "You cannot *imagine* how dearly I love every one of the family—nor can I say in words how dearly," runs one letter composed in 1843. "I assure you, my dear Father, that my eyes run over with tears often and often when some passing recollection of misconduct on my own part, in our old domestic relations, comes into my mind. I would give a great part of all that I hope for in this world if I could say that I had never pained your heart, or shown temper to my dearest Mother, or tyrannized over the boys, or offended Aunt."[8] But there

---

8. Cooke Collection. Letter dated Martinsburg, April 26, 1843.

is nothing here to suggest, in domestic relations, more than might be expected from a sensitive, high-spirited youth galled by bondage to a profession he did not like and tormented by the charms of a fascinating cousin. For the most part, the course of family life at Glengary must have been for him not much less bright and satisfying than it seemed years later in the memory of his brother:

"My first recollection of my Father," reads an early passage in John Esten's fragmentary manuscript autobiography, "shows him on horseback coming from Winchester, and telling me that 'no humming tops could be had' . . . but giving me a common top which I was soon spinning in the upper passage near the book-case. . . . My dearest Mother I recollect in those days as an emanation from some higher place, a something bright and beautiful which watched over me day and night: Pa was rather a dignified and most affectionate being of superior nature to the rest of the world, who gave me all I wished or capriced in the wide world and never thwarted my desires. . . . I recollect well Brother Philip as a great hunter before the Lord, and walking in his dressing gown from his grove-study. I think I recollect his marriage, and his delicate black mustache. His noble voice and dark eyes I could not fail to mark. Sister Willie in due time came—the autumn I think, of 1837—and I recollect Sal kept long a beautiful geranium for the new sister.

"I remember—how distinctly—Brother Ed's little poney coming galloping out of town:— . . . and our burying apples in the grove, white small apples in the brown soft earth!— the earth smell and flavor is, now, how plain to me!—under the ash tree:—and Brother Phil's burying Milo his pointer, shot by accident, under the big oak in the woods, and firing over him—the poor dead and gone pointer-emperor, a salute:— . . . and seeing Brother shooting bats from the front porch in the still evening when the sun was dying 'over the hills and far away':— . . . and Brother Phil's deer coming home in a cart, killed at eighty yards with a ball under the eye and falling back into a covey of partridges:— . . . and hearing Brother Phil's Aeolian harp while Wm. was putting on wood in his little grove study:— and his figured dressing gown: . . . .

"Further I recall the scenery of the Glengary kitchen with its ebon forms, in which I have since located the caliph, and fisherman and wondrous fishes of the 'Arabian Nights': and the long-necked Indian hen Brother brought in behind the stable: and the great tulip tree beneath the tall hill 'from which' they said 'you might see Harper's Ferry. . . .'

"Sister Willie too to my childish imagination was some rare being come from fairy land—a flower, a picture, something pretty and fresh. This impression must have been more vivid from the fact that she used to go on long rambles with us in the grove. . . .

"We left Glengary for Charlestown in the summer of '38 or '39 and came to 'dwell within the strangers' land' here in the lowlands, in course of time. Certes I love the lowcountry, and all my heart is with my friends so well-loved: —but I cling obstinately to my childhood in the upper country still. . . ."[9]

From these childhood memories of John Esten Cooke it appears that the elder brother had already developed that skill with rifle and musket which later was to earn him the reputation of being perhaps the most accomplished hunter in a region traditionally noted for its addiction to field sports. The hillsides and forests near Glengary provided ample opportunity for exercise with the gun. Indeed, the whole lower Shenandoah Valley abounded with small game; and beyond the Alleghanies, in the Blackwater coun-

---

9. John Esten Cooke, Personal Recollections of John Esten Cooke, The Younger. A manuscript in the possession of Dr. R. P. Cooke.

try or along Lost River,[10] a catamount or a brown bear was now and then to be met with. One record of Cooke's hunting has been preserved, in his own handwriting. It is merely an itemized list of small game killed or snared during the month of October, 1845, and it says nothing of his prowess in the more arduous forms of the sport. But, as John Esten Cooke observes, the quantity of ducks, pheasants, partridges, turkeys, and so on, would astound a city sportsman.[11]

Too, there were relatives and friends comfortably established on estates not too remote, among whom not a few had tastes akin to the tastes of Cooke, if not so consuming as his. By his own testimony some of them rivaled him in certain branches of the manly art. His passion for turkey-hunting, and all the skill he possessed in that art, he declared in the sketch "The Turkey-Hunter in His Closet,"[12] grew out of his association with two gentlemen nearly of his own age, and closely related to him in blood. One of them was so inveterate a hunter of that particular game, that his friends called him "Turkey-Foot." And Pendleton Kennedy, perhaps one of the two, testified that:

"Like the valiant Sir Thomas Erpingham in France, he was

'Very fatal in the field.'

Almost innumerable wild turkeys and pheasants, ducks, hares, partridges—to say nothing of the deer—has he slain in his time,—and a very hearty trencherman was he, too, in helping to consume them. Before yet the faintest dull grey streak had appeared in the dawn, he has breasted the steep hill-sides of the forest—no dainty huntsman; but a bold

---

10. Both in what was then western Virginia, now West Virginia. That Cooke was familiar with the region is indicated by descriptions in his *John Carper, The Hunter of Lost River* and by other evidences scattered through his letters.
11. "Recollections," *Messenger*, XXVI, 427.
12. *Messenger*, XVII (October-November, 1851), 659. Posthumously published.

and courageous one, that would meet the hoar-frost with rapture, and feel an unusual thrill at his heart when the snows were deepest, and the streams most glassed in ice:—and let him but once get upon the tracks of his game, and the oldest, most trained and regularly bred hunter of the hills, was not keener in the pursuit—and he was durable, too, as a hound:—I have known him cross the streams waist-deep when the waters were almost frozen, and shake himself dripping on the opposite bank with a wild delight, that was almost savage. In the Fall and Winter the forests were as familiar to him as his own parlour. He loved their wild recesses, and knew all their points of beauty—where the sun broke the grandest upon them in the morning, and where the dying rays fell saddest and sweetest upon their hidden vales. . . . His imagination was all alive in the dim and shadowy forests, and bold mountains around where he dwelt; and the poetry of his nature was all astir in him, when he frequented their untrodden wilds. And hence came some of the best inspiration of his poetry—the most thoughtfully dwelt upon—the truest to nature, and with more too of his real soul in them."[13]

To John Esten Cooke, though more sedate in temper and far less the sportsman than his poet-brother, the social aspects of the latter's life at Glengary seemed worthy of a canvas not entirely deficient, he believed, in interest. On it would figure very many gay festivals and country frolics —fishing parties of young men and maidens, wandering at ease along the banks of the beautiful streams, or sailing in the boat which gently rocked today upon the current, under the great willow shadowing the Opequon, as in other years —gay riding parties, too, galloping through the spring or autumn woods—the time enlivened by the smiles of ladies fair—by many a jest, and by joyous laughter long since

13. Kennedy Memoir.

hushed, but ringing still in the memories and hearts of those who remained to read those lines—night-hunting with hounds, or with the spear used in transfixing fish seen by the light of the blazing torch—horse races—country weddings where, to the merry violin, the joyous reel went on its way in triumph, and the festival was kept up, without flagging, day after day and night after night. These, and "a hundred other scenes" of his brother's youth and his own, might he describe.[14]

Cooke's marriage to Willianne Corbin Tayloe Burwell[15] on May 1, 1837, promised no cessation to the cavalier life so glowingly pictured by the memory of John Esten Cooke. A daughter of William Nelson Burwell of "Glenowen," and a descendant of Robert "King" Carter of "Corotoman," she had lived at "Saratoga" with an uncle, Nathaniel Burwell, who had adopted her after her father's death. She is described as having great personal beauty and charm of manner—the descriptive lines in Cooke's poem, "Emily," undoubtedly refer to her—and attendance at the academy for young ladies conducted by Miss Margaret Mercer at "Bellemonte" had added the cultural graces considered appropriate to an heiress and maiden of nineteen. After marriage, she went to live at Glengary as "Sister Willie," the "rare being come from fairy land," of John Esten Cooke's recollections. Her quiet cheerfulness and strength of character were to serve her husband in good stead during the troubled years that lay ahead.[16]

14. "Recollections," *Messenger*, XXVI, 424.
15. The name is variously given: Willie Anne Burwell, Anne Burwell, Anne Tayloe Burwell, Anne Corbin Tayloe Burwell, in which last form it appears in "The Cemetery Record," *Old Chapel, Clarke County, Virginia.*
16. On July 22, 1838, her first child, Elizabeth Lewis, was born. The birth of two other daughters—Maria Pendleton, on April 15, 1840, and Nancy Burwell, on April 27, 1843—preceded the birth of a son, Nathaniel Burwell, on April 24, 1845. The last child, Alethea Collins, was born on January 23, 1848, just two years before the death of its father. To all of them Mrs. Cooke was the devoted mother; to Cooke, the devoted wife. Soon after her marriage,

blindness began to develop—perhaps as the result of eye-strain during her schooldays following an attack of measles. By the early sixties she could scarcely see. One of her rare letters, to her brother-in-law John Esten Cooke, is written in such a sprawling, uncertain hand as a blind person might learn to make. But no one who had not been told of her infirmity could have guessed it from her manner. She lived on after her husband's death at the "Vineyard" (the country estate near Millwood, Clarke County, Virginia—twelve miles from Winchester, where the last years of Cooke's life were spent) with her first- and third-born children, who never married. Those who remember her later years picture her as a rarely beautiful, stately old lady, knitting in an arm-chair while the daughters read to her, or absent-mindedly fingering the great keys in the key basket on her lap. She died at the Vineyard on November 23, 1899.

CHAPTER IV

Martinsburg, the West, and the Law

AT THE AGE of twenty-one Philip Pendleton Cooke had attained a status which to his contemporaries must have seemed exceptional, for at his death all but the briefest obituary notices mentioned it. He was married. He had been admitted to the practice of law in the courts of Virginia. He had acquired a reputation as a gentleman-poet and essayist for whom the prospects for fame were bright. And he was coming to be known, if not already known, as the best hunter in the Shenandoah Valley, a Nimrod without peer.

Other gentlemen might be practicing lawyers and family men at twenty-one. Others still might be accomplished scribblers or indefatigable hunters. But in few others, if any, of Cooke's generation did this combination of achievements occur. For the memory of Cooke the combination has proved unfortunate. Its unusual and romantic features attracted the notice of his contemporaries; and literary historians, leaning upon tradition, have tended to emphasize the exceptional, to the neglect of the impressive, if slender, body of work Cooke accomplished during the last few years of his life.

To Cooke himself, his status doubtless seemed not unworthy of pride, but hardly one to be continued. His letter to Tucker, quoted above, reveals that he had resolved late in 1835 to forsake literature as a calling; and after the *Messenger* contributions during the first half of 1836, the resolution evidently was given effect. For the year 1837 there is no surviving work that without question can be credited to him. For the year 1838 remain a carriers' address, a lament inspired by the death of a relative, and two other occasional poems contributed to the *Messenger*.[1] Nothing was published in 1839.

Late in that year, encouraged by Edgar Allan Poe, Cooke's desire for a literary career revived for a time; and in 1840 he published two of his best poems (both of which, however, were composed earlier). But for the years 1841 and 1842 the record is blank. In 1843 his poetic vein was reopened, and two of Cooke's most graceful poems, "Life in the Autumn Woods" and "Power of the Bards," appeared in the *Messenger*. But for 1844 the record is again blank, and so it remains for almost the whole of 1845. In fact, to the last four years of Cooke's life belong most of his prose works that deserve to be remembered, and perhaps the majority of his poems.

The years between the marriage of Cooke and Willianne Burwell and their removal in 1845 to the "Vineyard" estate were not, however, to be devoted consistently, or profitably, to the practice of law. The beginning seems to have been auspicious enough. Living with the family at Glengary, Cooke continued to aid his father in the preparation of legal cases and in the management of the estate. Presumably, too, he now and then conducted a case for himself at Winchester, or at Berryville in the courts of the new county, Clarke, which had just been formed from the eastern half of Frederick. But there began, in 1838, a series of family and personal misfortunes only obscurely reflected in surviving records but drastic in their effect upon both father and son.

1. "Carriers' Address," "How Sleeps My Friend," "On Dreaming I Heard a Lady Engaged in Prayer," and "To Mary." The last two are probably Cooke's although they cannot be positively identified.

Financial reverses may have had their origin in the guilelessness of the elder Cooke, who could not resist the requests of friends and associates to endorse their notes. When the panic of 1837, followed by severe depression, thrust upon him unanticipated legal obligations, his own family suffered in order that honor might be upheld. Moreover, in 1835 Cooke had embarked with his brother-in-law—Judge Philip C. Pendleton, of Martinsburg—and John Pendleton Kennedy, upon an extensive coal-mining venture in which other relatives, including Philip Pendleton Cooke, were also to some extent involved. For the Cookes the venture was unprofitable. The property ultimately came into the joint possession of Judge Pendleton, Kennedy, and Kennedy's father-in-law, Edward Gray, a wealthy textile operator and financier of Baltimore.[2]

In the late summer of 1838 the serious state of his affairs determined John R. Cooke to sell Glengary and move with his family to Baltimore. The plan, however, was not carried out. Early in 1839 Glengary was destroyed by fire, and the Cookes moved to Charlestown. There the family stayed until March, 1840. John R. Cooke then settled in Richmond in order to rebuild his fortunes through practice at the bar in the capital of the state.[3] Philip, with his own growing family, remained for some months in Charlestown to await what time and a yet-to-be-established legal practice might produce.

To what extent Philip Pendleton Cooke had been per-

2. For an extended discussion of the elder Cooke's financial fortunes and of his relations with John Pendleton Kennedy, see the author's dissertation.
3. He was only moderately successful, though at his death he was still esteemed as a leading member of the Virginia bar. For example, the Richmond *Daily Dispatch* for December 18, 1854, spoke of him as one who had been "a bright and conspicuous ornament" of his profession, of whose talents as a lawyer "John Randolph had an exalted opinion . . . and so expressed himself, in very strong terms." His wife, who for many years had been in feeble health, died on March 12, 1850, scarcely two months after the death of her eldest son.

sonally involved in the reverses of his father cannot be safely inferred from the evidence, which does, however, establish the fact that he had endorsed the latter's notes. Family tradition says that, irritated by this display of loyalty (a loyalty which, it would seem, placed in jeopardy the inheritance of Willianne Burwell Cooke), Nathaniel Burwell separated husband and wife and carried the latter away to live at Saratoga. The tradition probably is well founded, but the event, it would appear from passages in Cooke's correspondence, hardly could have happened before 1840.

In the meantime Cooke had received a letter from Edgar Allan Poe, who had been connected with the *Messenger* during the period of Cooke's contributions and who, since July, 1839, had been co-editor with William E. Burton of the *Gentleman's Magazine* in Philadelphia. Poe's letter is not extant. The general nature of its contents, however, can be inferred from Cooke's reply.

He had received Poe's friendly letter a long time ago, he wrote, but had scarcely been at home since its receipt. His wife had enticed him off to visit her kindred in the country, and he had seen more of guns and horses and dogs than of pens and paper. Amongst dinners, barbecues, snipe shooting, riding parties, and the like he could not gain his brains into the humor for writing to Poe, or to anybody else. He had reached home two days ago, and now hastened to assure Poe of his undiminished regard and respect, and to tell him the reasons of his neglect in leaving a letter so long unanswered. He then turns to their work:

"I do not believe you ingenuous or sincere when you speak in the terms which you use touching the value of my rambling compositions—my contributions to the Messenger &c—yet it of course cannot be disagreeable to me to find myself considered worth flattering. I will send you occasionally—if possible—such matters as I may consider worth inserting in the Gentleman's Magazine with pleasure; I cannot promise anything like the systematic contribution which I was guilty of in White's case, for the 'madness of scribbling' which once itched and tickled at my fingers-ends has been considerably cured by a profession and matrimony—money-cares and domestic squabbles—buying beef and mutton, and curing my child's croups, colicks, &c. The fever with which I was afflicted has given way to a chill—or, as romantic young persons say, 'The golden dream is broken.'

"As to *Ligeia*, of which you ask my opinion, (doubtless without any intention of being guided by any person's but your own) I think it very fine. There is nothing *unintelligible* to my mind in the 'sequel' (or conclusion) but I am impertinent enough to think that it (the conclusion) might be mended. I of course 'took' your 'idea' throughout. The whole piece is but a sermon from the text of 'Joseph Glanvil' which you cap it with—and your intent is to tell a tale of the 'mighty will' contending with and finally vanquishing Death. The struggle is vigorously described—and I appreciated every sentence as I advanced, until the Lady Ligeia takes possession of the deserted *quarters* (I write like a butcher) of the Lady Rowena. There I was shocked by a violation of the ghostly proprieties—so to speak—and wondered how the Lady Ligeia—a wandering essence—could, in quickening *the body of the Lady Rowena* (such is the idea) become suddenly the visible, bodily Ligeia. If Rowena's bodily form had been retained as a shell or case for the disembodied Lady Ligeia, and you had only become aware *gradually* that the blue Saxon eye of the 'Lady Rowena of Tremaine' grew daily darker with the peculiar, intense expression of the 'look' which had belonged to Ligeia—that a mind of grander powers, a soul of more glowing fires occupied the quickened body and gave an old familiar expression to its motions—if you had brooded and meditated upon the change until proof accumulated upon proof, making wonder certainty, and then, in the moment of some strangest of all evidence of the transition, broken out into the exclamation which ends the story—the *effect* would not have been lessened, and the 'ghostly proprieties' would, I think, have been better observed. You may have some theory of the story, or transition, however, which I have not caught.

"As for your compositions of this class, generally, I consider them, as Mr. Crummles would say, 'phenomenous.' You *write* as I sometimes *dream* when asleep on a heavy supper (not heavy enough for nightmare).—The odd ignorance of the name, lineage, &c. of Ligeia—of the circumstances, place, &c. under which, and where, you first saw her—with which you begin your narrative, is usual, and not at all wondered at, in dreams. Such dimness of recollection does not *whilst we dream* excite any surprise or diminish the *vraisemblable* aspect of the strange matters that we dream of. It is only when we wake that we wonder that so material an omission in the thread of the events should have been unnoticed by the mind at a time when it could dream in other respects so plausibly—with such detailed minuteness—with such self-possession.

"But I must come to a conclusion, as I tire myself with this out-of-the-way sort of writing.

"I will subscribe to the Gentleman's Magazine shortly and also 'contribute' to it.

"P.S.—I would not say *'saith Lord Verulam'*—it is out of the way. I am very impertinent."[4]

_{4. From the original in the Griswold Collection, dated Charlestown, Sept. 16, 1839. Cooke's letter and Poe's answer appear in *Edgar Allan Poe, Complete Works*, Virginia Edition, ed. by James A. Harrison, New York, 1902, pp. 49-54, and also in many of the fuller collections of Poe's works or studies of his life.}

_{The postscript to Cooke's letter obviously alludes, as Poe's answer renders certain, to the original form of a passage in the second paragraph of "Ligeia,"}

In answer to Cooke's letter, which he had just received and had read "with more pleasure than I can well express," Poe gave assurance that no flattery had been intended in his praise of Cooke's early contributions to the *Messenger:* "I have an inveterate habit of speaking the truth—and had I not valued your opinion more highly than that of any man in America I should not have written you as I did.

"I say that I read your letter with delight. In fact I am aware of no delight greater than that of feeling one's self appreciated (in such wild matters as 'Ligeia') by those in whose judgment one has faith. You read my most intimate spirit 'like a book,' and with the single exception of D'Israeli, I have had communication with no other person who does. Willis had a glimpse of it—Judge Tucker saw about one half way through—but your ideas are the very echo of my own. I am very far from meaning to flatter—I am flattered and honored. Beside me is now lying a letter from Washington Irving in which he speaks with enthusiasm of a late tale of mine, 'The Fall of the House of Usher,'—and in which he promises to make his opinion public, upon the first opportunity,—but from the bottom of my heart I assure you, I regard his best word as but dust in the balance when weighed with those discriminating opinions of your own, which teach me that you feel and perceive."

Poe was sending numbers of the *Gentleman's Magazine,* but Cooke should not think of subscribing, for the criticisms were not worth his notice.

It made him laugh, he concluded, to hear Cooke speaking about "romantic young persons" as of "a race with whom, for the future, you have nothing to do. You need not attempt to shake off or to banter off Romance. It is an

---

which in definitive editions reads: " 'There is no exquisite beauty,' says Bacon, Lord Verulam, speaking truly of all the forms and *genera* of beauty, 'without some *strangeness* in the proportion.' "

evil you will never get rid of to the end of your days. It is a part of yourself—a portion of your soul. Age will only mellow it a little, and give it a holier tone. I will give your contributions a hearty welcome, and the choicest position in the magazine."[5]

After a delay of three months, Cooke again found time for correspondence with Poe. He must not expect Cooke to make of him an exception among correspondents by writing to him punctually. Nor should Poe suspect the nature of Cooke's feeling toward him because of failure to be punctual. He had read Poe's "Fall of the House of Usher," his "William Wilson," and his "Conversation of Eiros and Charmion," and, as all authors liked praise and compliment, he would say something about them:

"In the first place I must tell you (what I firmly believe) that your mere style is the very best amongst the first of the living writers; and I must let you know that I regard style as something more than the mere manner of communicating ideas. 'Words are used by the wise as counters; by the foolish as coin,' is the aphorism of a person who never appreciated Jeremy Taylor or Sir Thomas Browne. You do not, to be sure, use your words as those fine old glowing rhetoricians did, as tints of the pencil—as the colours of a picture—you do not make your sentences pictures—but you mould them into an artful excellence—bestow a care which is pleasantly perceptible, and accomplish an effect which I can only characterize as the visible presentation of your ideas instead of the mere expression of them.

"In your 'Fall of the House of Usher,' unconnected with style, I think you very happy in that part where you prolong the scene with Roderick Usher after the death of his sister; and the glare of the moon thro' the sundering house, and the

---

5. From the original in the Griswold Collection. Letter dated September 21, 1839.

electric gleam visible around it, I think admirably conceived.

"Of 'William Wilson' I am not sure that I perceive the true clew. From the 'Whispering Voice' I would apprehend that you meant the second William Wilson as an embodying of the *conscience* of the first; but I am inclined to the notion that your intention was to convey the wilder idea that every mortal of us is attended with a shadow of himself—a duplicate of his own peculiar organization—differing from himself only in a certain angelic taint of the compound, derived from heaven, as our own wild humours are derived from Hell (figuratively);—I cannot make myself understood, as I am not used to the expression of a wild *half thought*. But, although I do not clearly comprehend, I certainly admire the story.

"Of 'Eiros and Charmion' I will only say that I consider the whole very singular and excellent, and the skill of one small part of it unapproachable.

"'Was I much mourned, my Eiros'—is one of the finest touches in the world. ... The Poetry headed 'The Haunted Palace' which I read in the Baltimore Museum where it first appeared, and which I instantly understood as a picture of an intellect, I consider beautiful but grotesque.

"By the way you have selected an excellent title for your volume of Tales. 'Tales of the grotesque and the Arabesque' expresses admirably the character of your wild stories—and as Tales of the grotesque and arabesque they were certainly never equalled.

"I am writing a Book which I call *'Maurice Weterbern'*—what it is you will some time or other see. I am bestowing great *care* but little *labour,* upon it.

"I send you two pieces of verse (*Poetry* I dare not call them) which I made a year ago. If you think them worth

Martinsburg, the West, and the Law 47

publishing publish them—if not I am too hacknied to consider your decision an affront."[6]

Cooke's readiness to contribute to Burton's *Gentlemen's Magazine* and the closing paragraphs of his second letter to Poe reveal the inability of the law, family misfortunes, and domestic duties wholly to conquer the impulses of his native talent. True, "Maurice Weterbern" continued to be the object of little labor.[7] Nor, after sending the "two pieces of verse" which he had made "a year ago," did Cooke further contribute to the *Gentleman's Magazine*. The two—"Florence Vane" and "Earl March"—were published in the February and March numbers of 1840. With the June number Poe's connection with the magazine ended. Had Poe remained with Burton, his encouragement might have elicited from Cooke a volume and a quality of contributions which would have importantly affected the contemporary and posthumous estimates of his significance.

On the other hand, so inconstant was the state of Cooke's affairs during the early eighteen-forties, and so troubled was the state of his spirit, that perhaps no amount of editorial stimulus from Poe could have accomplished much. Heretofore Cooke had depended upon his father for a life of ease, not to say luxury. Now, reduced to relative poverty, he found himself the responsible head of a family whose income must be produced mainly by his own efforts. Those efforts might be supplemented, now and then, by small sums of money from his father,[8] and by the meager, uncertain

6. From the original in the Griswold Collection. Letter dated Charlestown, Jefferson County, Virginia, December 19, 1839. This letter seems to have been overlooked by some of Poe's biographers. Hervey Allen, for example, in his *Israfel, The Life and Times of Edgar Allan Poe*, p. 458, gives two paragraphs to Cooke's letter of September 16, but fails to mention the later one.

7. The work was never completed, and there is no evidence that Cooke carried it beyond the initial stage of planning. *The Chevalier Merlin*, however, Cooke's unfinished novel which appeared serially in the *Messenger* ten years later, may have grown out of the original conception.

8. Cooke's letters to his father during this period frequently mention such

return from his wife's inheritance, still administered by her uncle and guardian, Nathaniel Burwell. Large enough to support his family in comfort, Cooke's income certainly was not.

Faced with this problem, Cooke had the choice of certain alternative procedures. He might migrate to the West, where thousands of young Virginians—and particularly under the spur of the depression years—had already preceded him. He might hang out his shingle in Charlestown, or Martinsburg, or some other town in the Valley that could offer employment to a gentleman-lawyer. He might attempt to win fame and fortune in a political career. He might remove to Richmond, where his father, too optimistic regarding his own prospects, shortly was urging him to come. Or, living with relatives, he might simply await the day when, time and tactfulness having mollified Mr. Burwell, Cooke's wife would come into her inheritance and the family could settle down on a country estate. Meanwhile, he might find such diversions as his gun and country frolics could provide; and when the humor came he might compose poems, or perhaps a novel, though of profit from literary activity he had little expectation.

Of these various plans, Cooke preferred the first. For a time circumstances forced on him the second. But, in effect, the last is the one he followed; for his aversion for the law and his fondness for the chase were too strong to permit success at a calling which even in prosperous years required habits and inclinations he did not possess.[9]

An exploratory trip to the West, preliminary to ultimate

---

sums, though it is not apparent that they were gifts from the elder man. Perhaps they represented the desire of the father to indemnify, out of his own modest resources, the son for losses suffered in connection with the former's investments.

9. Cooke's movements during this period are discussed at length in the author's dissertation, where extensive use is made of the extant letters from Cooke to his father during the decade 1840-1850. The letters are particularly rich for the first half-decade.

removal, was projected for April of 1840.[10] It was not, however, to occur until the following year. Perhaps inability to obtain traveling funds prevented; perhaps objection on the part of Mr. Burwell to migration of his niece to faraway Missouri; perhaps the condition of Mrs. Cooke, who on April 15, 1840, gave birth to her second daughter. At any rate, not until August, 1841, was Cooke able to write his father:

"I have returned from my journey with my plans matured—and everything fair before me. . . . I have fixed on Palmyra in Marion Co., Mo. as my place of residence. It is healthy, full of business, and a *Whig* town in a Whig county. I became acquainted with every body worth knowing in the town, and made an *impression*. They urged me to 'come out'—promised me business—and to send me to the Legislature as soon as I made a good speech. Wright, a lawyer there, told me I could live like a *frugal* gentleman there for $500 per annum;—that his friend Mr. So and So, a lawyer with a wife and three children, rented his house and hired his servants and yet lived *within* $500 per annum. I can get a nice cottage establishment for $100 per annum; and, if I choose, the finest residence (a really elegant establishment) in the place, for $150 per annum. I will take out servants. My funds will be abundant *next Spring* for my removal, etc. I will not go until then. I have some Mo. Law Books which I must digest thoroughly along with Blackstone and Chilty's Pleading, before I go—to say noth-

---

10. "I propose going to the west early in April *if possible*. Anne will house herself during my absence at Saratoga whither we have been invited. . . . *Anne loves you all* with an affection greatly matured by our recent and long sojourn together. She says she 'will not' go to Missouri without first visiting you in Richmond. I do not know, however, that *she* will make the visit (money is too scarce with us all for such jaunts) but *I* will most certainly visit you before my final removal. I *rely* upon your success and prosperity and look with confidence to bright and famous new days for both of us."—From a letter dated Sunday, March 22, 1840, in the possession of the author. The letter was composed in Charlestown, where Cooke was still residing.

ing of other reasons for delaying removal. Love to Ma in quantities. I will write again before many days. We will spend the fall and winter in Martinsburg again. I left Anne in Clarke yesterday. She had just got a letter from Ma, and was much gratified. I have been back 9 days."[11]

Cooke was never, in fact, to represent Palmyra in the legislature nor to make a speech to its Whig citizens. The purpose to emigrate, however, persisted in his mind, even after a change in prospects made emigration seem less attractive as a solution to his problems. Nor was his exploratory journey wholly without result. Scenes and characters in one of his novelettes[12] plainly reflect impressions gathered during the journey from Virginia to Missouri and return.

In the meantime the Cookes had taken up residence in Martinsburg, where for four years Cooke was to spend such time in the practice of law as was not spent in other fashion elsewhere. A letter to his father late in December records that he had been away from Martinsburg six weeks. His family had been weather-bound in Charlestown on their return from Saratoga, reaching Charlestown early on the first day of the great snowfall. He had been in the woods daily for three weeks (Sundays excepted) with Stephen Dandridge, turkey-shooting. He had, however, in the same time read a great deal—the second and third volumes of Scott's *Life of Napoleon,* among other things. He read every afternoon about three hours and as many hours after bedtime (eight o'clock) nightly. He thought Scott's work the grandest book of the nineteenth century; he had always heard that it was unworthy of its author. His mawkish friends (Napoleon's) said the book was one-sided and prejudiced; but he was sure, for one, that it gave a nobler view of the giant than any books of eulogy and lavish admiration

---

11. From the original in the possession of Miss Anne Meade. Undated.
12. *The Two Country Houses,* published in 1848, but begun in 1843 with the title "Mary Hunter of Cotsworth."

he had read; and he had read a good many. Scott's talent for romance writing had helped rather than injured the book. It had not tainted his narration of facts, but had enriched and made graceful the other duties of his task. Napoleon in Moscow looking from a window of the Kremlin upon the burning city and saying in an undertone "These be Scythians indeed," and in his flight muttering as he traced the course of the Beresina upon his maps (hunting out a passing place) "Ah! Charles the Swede—Pultowa!", becomes one of Scott's Romance Kings. We were made familiar not only with the broad views of the man, in this book, but with his poetic emotions.

He had read a good deal in the old *Edinburgh Reviews*, and, as the Roundhead preachers used to say, "to my edification and the comely growth of my grace." He now began reading Blackstone—the English original, not Tucker's—today. He would read it with a glance instead of a gaze. He wanted to get a bird's-eye view of the science (which habit, he trusted, would render pleasant to him as to any); and this he could not do if he loitered too much on parts.

He would certainly go to Missouri in the spring, and, as far as he could now judge, directly to Palmyra. There, if he concluded to cast anchor in that place, he would work out his fortunes yet, and the world should hear something of him. He was entirely without despondency or fear. His family had a decent living—economy could make a meager income go very far—in any event. All that he had to do was "to *increase their comforts* by adding to the plain necessaries of life its luxuries, the dessert of fair fruits to the dinner of beef and bacon."

The only black dog that haunted his steps was the fear that his father's death might throw his dear mother and the children on his shoulders before they were strong enough to support them. To be sure, he would dare all things for them, even batter his brains out against any wall that fortune might raise in his path toward their maintenance; but although he would sacrifice life itself, yet what would the sacrifice avail them?:

"It is, my dearest father, a terrible thing to mingle up with the awful idea of a dear and near one's death the painful and miserable reflections that I have, just now, been bold enough to speak out to your ear. Let Providence preserve you, the only present stay of the dear children and my mother, until I can build up my home in the bountiful West, and then with the blessing of the same Providence the honour and unsullied position of *our house* shall be left *intact* to the generation who in the nature of things will be their next guardians. It is lamentable to see the old families of the land, the first in gentility and *caste, reduced;* to see their descendants gradually sinking by marriage and association into humbler classes; and to see *mine* thus would break my heart. All this tends to what I have before urged on you. Insure your life—no matter for how small a sum. Two, three, five thousand dollars would be a buoy to them in case of your premature death. If you cannot spare the money requisite for effecting the insurance from your income, *borrow it*. Create a new debt rather than *run the great risque*.

"I have thought somewhat on another subject. Get over your repugnance to a West Point Education. Send Henry or John Esten to West Point. Get a situation for one *there,* and place the other in the Navy. . . . *The Bar* is a lottery. I earnestly entreat that you will not only think of this but consent to do it. The officers of the Army and Navy *are never outranked* in American society. The 'sailor,' besides, will see 'many countries' and have fair opportunities of observation, and if he should prove possessed of even my poor modicum of brains will make good literary use of his 'chances.' The young 'Lieutenant' will probably run no worse career than Uncle St. George is running—and *may* do greater things than Uncle has done. I *dream* of fighting my way into position (political) and it may be (stranger things have happened) that I shall be able on some day or other to do something towards their advancement. . . .

"Anne is well and in good spirits. She is my *comfort*. We love and know each other. My little girls are beautiful children. The youngest, Maria Pendleton, is full of life and merriment, and very much in face like Ma. Lizzy calls her 'Pennon' and is devoted to her. Liz. herself is, *I think*, the most perfect child I ever saw. . . .

"There were several reasons why Anne and I did not visit you this fall. One was the circumstance that Mr. N. Burwell would spend the winter in Richmond. Another that we had but an indifferent nurse. Another that I wish to live the life of a recluse in no city where I know so many people as I do in Richmond—(and my taste would lead me to adopt a recluse life for some years in any city).— Another, and the *least* powerful, reason, was the expense about which you have bothered yourself so needlessly. I have a fund in Wheeling which I could have anticipated (125 dols.) or I could have anticipated Anne's income.

"I will of course visit you before I go westward. I am impatient for a reunion however temporary."[13]

The genuineness of Cooke's desire to prepare himself for successful legal practice in the West—or in Virginia, if the still anticipated removal to Missouri should not take place— is attested by various passages in letters to his father, which also throw light on the character of his reading and the nature of his diversions. He had been studying law, he wrote in November, 1841, without any cessation six hours daily for eleven days past, and had got to the point of find-

13. Cooke Collection. Letter dated Martinsburg, Dec. 29, 1840.

ing study easy and grateful. He had not resumed his novel because his time was limited and there was law reading enough to fill it up. The éclat of a successful novel would be a great adjunct, but a certain knowledge of pleading and of statute law was *essential* to his success in the West. Besides he had not become sufficiently engrossed in the study of law to make it safe for him to venture upon so satisfying an occupation as that of imagining the details of a showy and gorgeous romance; "I might be led *completely* and *exclusively* into the literary work...." Above all, it was a paramount duty to give Anne some of his waking hours; and, going to his studies at nine o'clock to leave them at half after four, having no interval but an hour for dinner, he left her few enough of them. He took notes as he read and mastered sixty pages every day, perfectly. The novel should, however, be written, and that before long; and he meant to lay himself out upon it.

He was as regular in attendance at his office as any man could be, and was in high spirits at having proved to himself that he could go resolutely to work.

His night reading, a postscript informed, was "the Newspapers, Froissart, Geological works, and Lewis and Clarke's expedition to the Pacific." This last work had interested him so much that he had read it, two large, full volumes, in six nights. He had finished it last night.[14]

Cooke's creditors, meanwhile, had brought bankruptcy proceedings, and a judgment had been given against him. The episode was a severe blow to his sensitive spirit. He was not, however, of a temperament that could be permanently depressed; moreover, he was beginning to see a present alternative for the Palmyra project; and in June, 1842, he wrote once again in cheerful vein to his father:

[14]. From the original in the possession of Miss Mariah P. Duval. Letter dated November 17, 1841.

"I returned here, yesterday, from a visit to the Bower and Martinsburg. Uncle Phil stirred me up like a trumpet with his 'fair imaginings' of my futurity. He would have persuaded me, if the great worldly rebuke which I have sustained had not blunted the edge of my hope somewhat, that there was nothing beyond my reach. He advises me to study law with earnest industry for one year—to practise it as much as I can—to speak on all occasions—in a word to fit myself for a political life:—and five or six years hence (on the death of a certain person) to go to Missouri. He calls Mo. the 'greatest theatre for talent in the Union.' You will find in my letter of the 26th. (what I repeat thro' fear that letter miscarried,) that Mr. B. is to build a house on Anne's land and give us $500 per year—with perquisites &c. Since seeing Uncle Phil I have resolved to spend the time between Sept. 1st and the completion of the house, in Battletown—boarding with my family and practising law. I will want the loan of *a few* of your books. I feel my spirit springing up from its long sleep like Iamblichus from his 'cave of slumber.' I will make the spoon yet—and it shall be of *silver*. Wealth is now the great mark at which I aim; the nobler mark at which I once aimed may be hit by the same shaft for '*Wealth and Fame lie in the same line.*' *I will study law for one year*—my motto shall be '*La fin couronne les œuvres*'—and I will *make* the great end. You will find my whole nature changed, and you will see these things *set about and persisted in*. Let me know the amount of my remaining responsibility for you; furnish me with *statements* in all cases of *usury* &c. &c. Insure your life if even for only two or three thousands. Remember me tenderly to Ma and the others. Write at once. God bless you. Anne is at Saratoga. All are well."[15]

15. Cooke Collection. Letter dated "Cassilis, Thursday." The approximate date of the letter is fixed by internal evidence and by passages in other letters. "Cassilis" was the country seat of Cooke's Kennedy kin, near Charlestown; and

Some months later Cooke was again moved to reassure his father regarding his constancy toward his profession. His life was an even current at present, he wrote. He discharged the duties of his life and position soberly and discreetly; was punctual in attendance at his office, studied law points, wrote, read, and did not hunt there or drink spirit. About once in ten days he spent a day in shooting with Stephen Dandridge. His health, accustomed as he was to a great deal of exercise, required that much. But it must not be inferred from this that his passion for shooting continued to be strong upon him. "It was only an evening or two ago, that old 'Uncle Charley' Stewart, with whom I was walking, said 'I reckon you can't stand walking as well as you could before you stopped hunting.' When people like him begin to talk of my shooting propensities, or of the indulgence of them, as matter of the past, it is a good sign."

Anne was well and looking "a really beautiful woman.... The children are well and winding themselves about old Mr. B.'s heart. I will go to housekeeping, and I am led to believe to *farming,* about the last of next summer.... Let me know if you are plagued by any of your old creditors. I desire to be kept *well informed* on this subject."[16]

Cooke's hopes regarding farming were not to be shortly realized. The house Mr. Burwell was building for Willianne rose no faster than the volume of Cooke's practice, and it was not occupied until the spring of 1845. For the present, Cooke continued to have "abundant leisure," although his condition in Martinsburg was "comfortable enough." He had, however, to be *"extremely* economical":

"The money you sent me I doled out, in payment of little debts &c., cent by cent, almost, and now have but twenty-

---

"Uncle Phil" was Philip C. Pendleton, Cooke's maternal uncle. "Battletown" was the original name of Berryville, county seat of Clarke. The evidence suggests that Cooke did not carry out his intention to settle there.

16. Miss Anne Meade. Letter dated October 20, 1842.

Martinsburg, the West, and the Law 57

five cents left. When I am to *make* money is a question which I cannot answer although I frequently ask it of myself. I find it as hard a task, and as difficult, as the alchymists did to transmute metals. I have been near making some several times but, as with them, the wonderful secret eluded me at the eleventh hour. I have already assured you, and now assure you again, that my greatest vexation in life is the not being able to do without your assistance in pecuniary matters. There is a striking and offensive impropriety in my taking my support, at twenty-six, from my father. The young of the eagles (of which high breed I persuade myself I am come) feed themselves when their wings are old enough. And so does every other animal, when matured, except that good for nothing creature a 'Virginia gentleman.' The only palliative of this still continuing (but surely soon to end) dependence on you is the strictest economy on my part, and that I will rigorously practise. This is a preface to my iteration of the cry of the horse leech's daughter 'give—give!' I want $2.00 to pay for a load of wood which I have bought this morning, $1.50 to pay to the farmer who winters my mare, about $1.00 to the saddler, and enough more to make up six or eight dollars altogether. My estimate which I sent you just before you remitted me the $25 was inaccurate to the extent I have just mentioned.

"How do you come on professionally? I bear in mind what you say concerning my ultimate removal to Richmond. It may very well come to pass that I will before very long practise law there with an income from lands and slaves in the valley to back me. I am sure that I will become very rich if I ever make $5000 per annum. I am as prudent in my expenditures as any man naturally liberal ever was."[17]

[17] Cooke Collection. Letter dated "Martinsburg, Nov: 28." The year was 1842.

The notion of settling in Richmond remained in Cooke's thoughts, as did the advice of his Uncle Phil to enter the political arena. But neither project came to anything. Mention of the former plan gradually dropped out of the correspondence between Cooke and his father. Pursuit of the political gleam prompted Cooke to make discreet inquiries of his cousin, John Pendleton Kennedy (then a member of Congress)—inquiries perhaps preliminary to an effort to obtain the post of United States district attorney for the Winchester area. And perhaps in pursuit of that goal, Cooke delivered in 1843 to the assembled commoners and gentry of Martinsburg a Fourth of July oration. It was, according to the Martinsburg *Gazette,* an excellent oration, "beautifully chaste in language, forcible and eloquent in style, and in every way adapted to give, as it did, universal satisfaction." The toast of "The Orator of the Day," too, was thought worthy of a conspicuous place among those that graced the account of the occasion: "The good old town of Martinsburg;—Receiving all the benefits of modern improvements, but not affected in her old fashioned propriety by their innovations."[18] Cooke's oratory, however, must have been too classically chaste and old-fashioned to win the genuine approval of a frontier democracy. At any rate, nothing more was heard of political ambitions.

Politics, Missouri, the new house that was slow in building, and the law had not wholly banished from Cooke's mind hope of achieving success with his pen. In April, 1843, he spoke of being engaged in writing "Ballads founded on some of the quaint narratives of 'The good knight John Froissart.'" There would be seven of them; he had advanced considerably in the work and composed "with surprising ease."[19] And "I mean to publish my Froissart Ballads before the Fall," he wrote in May to his father.

18. *Gazette,* July 6, 1843. The oration, in theme not unlike similar performances of the time, was worthy of the editor's adjectives.
19. Cooke Collection. Letter, Cooke to John R. Cooke, dated April 26, 1843.

His novel would succeed them without much of an interval. His delay in the execution of literary works, he believed, had arisen from a too great fastidiousness of taste, which made him look too carefully to what he wrote and checked the freedom of his composition. He had at last come to perceive that what he had most elaborated was not always his best work, and he meant "to write dashingly, and correct 'in the lump.' If I gain a present reputation I will spring at once into an enviable position. I will accomplish my destiny." As for what he had said earlier about Richmond and the bar, he still adhered to every purpose expressed in that letter, and was studying.[20]

The ballads based on Froissart are mentioned again in the fall, along with a new novel Cooke was writing.[21] "I send you two poems," he informed his father, "which I have written lately. Give them to Minor to be published in the Messenger. They may as well be published with my name to them as they are good enough for the latitude. But as *you* think.

"Tell Ma that she could not have struck my weak point better than in procuring the tomato and pumpkin seed for me. I shall be a notable gardener, and planter of trees and pruner of vines. The Vineyard shall, I am determined, be an abundant, nice, country seat. Ask her to keep the seeds dry, and not to *give away any of them*.

"Give my love to Aunt, Mary and the boys, and certainly to Aunt Giddy. Tell the boys that I hope great things of them—that is that I hope to see them useful, accomplished, and honourable gentlemen. The better books are the wells for them to draw from. Light, desultory reading, except to relieve the mind when it has been over-worked, is, I think, hurtful. . . . The best poetry of men like Milton, Wordsworth &c. is full of great truths, magnificently ut-

20. Cooke Collection. Letter dated May 17, 1843.
21. Given, in Cooke's letter, the title "Mary Hunter of Cotsworth," but ultimately published as *The Two Country Houses*.

tered; and the pomp of numbers sometimes inflames the mind when it would go to sleep over prose."[22]

The two poems that Cooke had sent to his father, "Life in the Autumn Woods" and "The Power of the Bards," show a decided improvement in quality over the work of his adolescence and early manhood. Two poetic modes had been conspicuous in Cooke's early verse: the lyric, and the narrative—more particularly, the narrative ballad. In work of both types he had displayed a strong feeling for nature and a fondness for heroic action, all too often overlaid, it must be admitted, with metaphysical obscurities or with juvenile imitations of the eighteenth-century English Romantics. Only to the extent that the earlier poems were free of such influences were they sucessful and worthy to be preserved.

Neither of the two poems that mark the re-awakening of Cooke's poetic talent reveals the characteristic blemishes of his juvenile efforts. They foreshadow the mode of his later poetry, the bulk of which was to be cast in the form of narrative embroidered with richly colored passages that reflect Cooke's abiding love of nature.

More popular than either "The Power of the Bards" or "Life in the Autumn Woods," although less important as poetry, was the composition Cooke alluded to in a letter to his father during the summer of 1844. Inspired by paternal affection, he had written a poem to his daughter and had sent it on to Richmond for the *Messenger*. Evidently the elder Cooke not only thought it unsuitable for publication but went on to speak unfavorably of the son's poetic endeavors.

"What you say about my poetic vein being exhausted," Cooke answered him, was a mistake. But "I agree with you

---

[22]. Miss Mariah P. Duval. Letter dated Martinsburg, October 13, 1843. Benjamin Blake Minor had succeeded White as editor of the *Messenger*. "Aunt Giddy" apparently was Cooke's Negro nurse during his infancy.

entirely, however, in believing that poetical composition gains a man neither wealth nor honours in this country. It is in the maturity of countries that the harp is listened to— or rather in the old age of countries, when energy has given way to ease and indulgence, and men have leisure to delight in the arts. The Anglo-Saxon who is pressing towards California with a knapsack on his back, has no leisure for scholarly indulgence; and he is a type of our population. I *know* that six months of continuous composition, such as that at Glengary in my nineteenth year, would develope my 'poetical vein'; and that any apparent poverty in its present yield is owing not to exhaustion but to the fact that the shaft has been, in years of disuse, choked with rubbish."

He had sent the verses addressed to his daughter because they were expressive of "a purified and chastened condition" of his inner man. He had striven for several years to weed his nature, to correct what, he painfully remembered, had embittered many an hour of the past when they were all together. And he thought his passions were more under his control, his charities more steady, his "domestic virtues (if I ever had any)" clearer than they were. The introduction of matters of his own private concern into the verses was natural in writing "*to* my little daughter—as I certainly *did* just as entirely, and as much without an eye to publication, as if I had been writing a letter to her." Having written in this unreserved way, however, he agreed, on reflection, that the verses ought not to be published. What his father said about prose was all true. It, after all, was the weapon for a stout-minded man; it did effective *work* in the world, and he meant to accomplish himself in its use if he could. Poetry would be only his occasional indulgence. He was a little ashamed to have written so much egotism.

"All are well," the letter continued. "I expect to go into the house presently. . . . I *will* pay my debts in time to prevent their oppressing me. I bear them now as I would a five pound weight." He had frequently been called on "to *speak* since the canvass began." He had always refused, but had consented to speak next week in the club house in Martinsburg.[23]

"To My Daughter Lily," the verses against whose publication John R. Cooke had counseled, was laid aside until November, 1845. Then, with other poems, it was sent for inclusion in a new edition of Griswold's *Poets and Poetry of America*. Griswold apparently found it unsuitable for the volume but arranged to have it published in the August, 1846, number of *Graham's Magazine*,[24] for which periodical he had served as literary editor. It was soon thereafter reprinted by a Baltimore newspaper;[25] and by 1847 it had even been taken up abroad—credited, however, to "G. Cooke, An American Poet."[26] By 1864 it had come to be thought of as one of those favorite poems that went the rounds of the weekly press "at least once a year."[27] Most of the biographical sketches of its author mention it and, with Painter, describe it as among his "choicest lyrics."[28] But notwithstanding its obvious appeal, "To My Daughter Lily" has more interest as autobiography than value as poetry. Its publication can be explained only through recognition that, in matters of propriety, the judgment of Cooke was sometimes less sound than that of his father. Its popularity can be explained only by reference to the prevailing sentimentality of the day.

23. Cooke Collection. Letter dated July 6, 1844. Available contemporary numbers of Martinsburg newspapers contain no information about the address, which perhaps was not made.
24. XXIX, 66. Signed "By P. P. Cooke, of Va."
25. *The Western Centinel*, Sept. 5, 1846.
26. *Chambers' Edinburgh Journal* (November 6, 1847), 304.
27. "Philip Pendleton Cooke," *The Knickerbocker Magazine*, LXIV (November, 1864), 426. Unsigned.
28. F. V. N. Painter, "Philip Pendleton Cooke," *Library of Southern Literature*, III, 1063.

CHAPTER V

The Vineyard and *Froissart Ballads*

SETTLEMENT at the Vineyard early in 1845 marked the beginning of the most productive years in the career of Philip Pendleton Cooke, and probably the most serene and happy period since his boyhood in Martinsburg and Winchester. Browsing in the Princeton library, composing romantic verses for the *Knickerbocker,* combining the pursuit of literature and the courtship of his cousin during the early years at Glengary, he had, indeed, known hours of happiness. But during the years that followed the scale swung heavily to the other side. Disappointment in love, the burning of Glengary, family misfortunes, bankruptcy, strained relations with his wife's uncle, and, all along, the practice of a profession he despised—against these must have seemed slight the pleasure derived from the chase, the country diversions in the company of his relatives, the rare literary employment of his pen. It is true that certain passages in the earlier letters to his father manifest a cheerful tone. They are to be considered, however, as expressing either the transient elevation of an impressionable poet natively healthy and hopeful of mind, or else the desire of a son to lighten his father's burdens by the assumption of an optimism he did not feel.

Removal to the Vineyard estate meant a new stage in the fortunes of Cooke, and a new vista of happiness. The security of his own family was now assured in so far as fertile acres could assure it. For a time, too, the outlook for his father's affairs bettered. The relations with Nathaniel Burwell eased. Cooke, it would appear, gave up serious thought of migrating to the West and settled down to enjoyment of Vineyard, occasional gentlemanly practice in the neighboring courts of law, hunting jaunts now and then with friends, and the serious pursuit of literature in several of its branches.

The house itself, the surroundings, and the location of the estate with reference to the scenes of Cooke's youth, all were such as to give pleasure to one of his temperament. A two-story brick structure, with sunny exposure looking eastward to the Blue Ridge and across the Valley to the Alleghanies, it stood on the summit of a spacious knoll two miles from the village of Millwood. Ample grounds for lawns, gardens, and orchard surrounded it. Behind, sloping down to the Shenandoah, distant only a short mile, grew a virgin forest where on any morning before sunrise Cooke might confidently expect to bag a turkey or, along the river bank, a brace of ducks. Far down in the foreground, and off to the left and right, a keen eye could make out the roofs of other country houses, and, farther away, "Carter Hall" in Millwood, Old Chapel (where gentry families worshiped and, in time, were buried) and on winter mornings, blue smoke from the chimneys of Winchester. Winchester was twelve miles away. Charlestown was only nineteen, and from there to Martinsburg was only fourteen. Within the quadrilateral formed by Millwood and these three, lived most of Cooke's relatives and friends.

Cooke's own satisfaction with his present status, dream though he might of a better, was expressed in the first letter he wrote to his father after moving to the Vineyard. Father and son, it reveals, had invested in Texas lands; payment for their respective shares was shortly to fall due; funds were not available. "By the way, the passage of the Texas Bill must have already rendered your whole interest more valuable than it was before; and if so, can you not sell a portion of it for the price you agreed to give for all, and so save the rest?"

He was, the letter continued, "as happy a man in my mere 'circumstances'—that is my 'surroundings' " as could be found anywhere. His house was good; his wife the most devoted, affectionate, and true creature in the world; his children sweet, obedient, healthy, good looking, and intelligent. He had all the comforts of life in sufficient abundance, and beyond them, habits of economy which would make one or two hundred dollars a year—a sum he could hope to earn—enough for all his extra indulgences. He had just begun gardening, and trimming up trees, and "you know how delightful such work is. Did we not enjoy it, in 'fates despite' at Glengary?—in old times?

"With the birds singing around my eaves, and my children, making merry out of doors and in, (I have grown very tolerant of noisy children) I am of course cheery and fresh at heart; but still even now I cannot wholly, nor can I ever, rid myself of the two troublesome griefs (if I may call them by so strong a name) which dash my cup. In the first place, you are struggling with the daily cares of life, and cannot be entirely happy. And, then, I am becalmed out of the current which the great world of men is moving onward upon; am sunk into inglorious quiet, whilst my temper is for action; am pruning trees, riding to a village to bring a plain action, or set aside an office judgment, reading books I have already read; and all this, and only this, whilst I incessantly hear internal voices that say 'Up—Up—the world is winning.' Your present cares, which thank God, you have a manly and heroic nature to encounter, give me most trouble. You *know,* my beloved Father, that I would leap into a gulph to rid you of them; and if you do not know, then let me tell you here once for all that I could *not consent to live* an hour after my conscience charged me with having preferred myself to you—my happiness to yours. You, from whom I draw my life, have bequeathed me much of your own high nature—if you had not done so, I might have looked without pain or grief, I might have looked in all the untroubled comfort of 'the wretch concentrated all in self,' on your cares which I cannot remove. I sometimes leap like a horse to the spur, when stung by this thought of your daily cares, and my own inaction, and then I take refuge in the dream that one day we may yet, God willing, stand shoulder to shoulder in some fair region of the South, and cheer each other and be happy together—we and ours."[1]

In the meantime, Cooke contented himself with the real satisfactions to be derived from employment with the affairs of the Vineyard. Actual management of the estate, more than a thousand acres in extent, apparently remained in the hands of Nathaniel Burwell until his death in November, 1849, two months before the death of Cooke. But to minister to a poet's taste for gardening there was ample space about the house. A memorandum in Cooke's own hand suggests the variety and strength of that taste. It records the planting of sixty-six fruit trees—peaches, pears, apples, and many others—no two of the same variety and each numbered and named in a neat column. Later entries note the progress of the trees and the planting of eighteen grape vines, with location of the vines indicated in a carefully drawn sketch.[2]

Composition could be among those satisfactions which might in time make a poet cease to think longingly of Missouri or of some fair region of the South. And he would

[1]. Miss Anne Meade. Letter dated "The Vineyard, Near Millwood, March 7, 1845." The outcome of the land venture cannot be determined, though available evidence suggests that for the Cookes the speculation proved unprofitable.
[2]. Manuscript in the possession of Mrs. Bevan.

resume this, and his legal study, Cooke informed his father in April, 1845, as soon as he got things tidy about him. A postscript added:

"Some of my long ago published pieces have lately taken a fresh start and I hear of them in different places republished with puffing flourishes."[3]

One of the pieces to which the postscript alludes doubtless was "Florence Vane," which Poe had praised strongly in a lecture in New York and then had republished in the *Broadway Journal* for March 15, 1845.[4] The event seems to have been significant for Cooke's future course. Late in the year, and throughout 1846, Rufus Griswold and John Pendleton Kennedy were to be useful in offering encouragement and in aiding in the preliminaries connected with the publication of Cooke's volume of verse. Without their aid, indeed, it may be questioned whether the volume could have appeared. The initial stimulus, however, to Cooke's poetic talent in the new and favorable environment of Vineyard seems to have come from Poe's lecture and his notice of Cooke in the *Broadway Journal*—a notice whose motive, perhaps, was merely to secure suitable material for the periodical with which the elder man had just become connected.

Whatever the motive, Poe's encouragement elicited a contribution from Cooke, a poem scarcely known today but deservedly ranked as one of his best. "The Mountains" appeared in the *Broadway Journal* for December 20.[5] One week later Poe referred to it in the editorial miscellany:

"The truly beautiful poem entitled 'The Mountains,' and published in our last Journal, will put every reader in mind of the terseness and severe beauty of Macaulay's best bal-

3. Cooke Collection. Letter dated April 28, 1845.
4. For an account of Poe's lecture and of his connection with the *Broadway Journal*, see John H. Ingram, *Edgar Allan Poe*, 291 ff.
5. II, No. 24, 368-69.

lads—while it surpasses any of them in grace and imagination. Not for years has so fine a poem been given to the American public. It is the composition of Mr. P. P. Cooke of Virginia, author of 'Florence Vane,' 'Young Rosalie Lee,' and other exquisitely graceful and delicate things. Mr. Cooke's prose, too, is nearly as meritorious as his poetry."[6]

Cooke's reputation had meanwhile come to the attention of Griswold, then engaged in preparing a new edition of his *Poets and Poetry of America;* and Kennedy, prompted by Griswold, set about securing from his cousin material suitable for the volume. The three-handed correspondence gives insight into Cooke's personality, his ambitions, and his plans. To a request from Kennedy he replied:

"I got your letter this morning and as the 8th of October is very near at hand I write at once to say that I will endeavour to do all you advise and ask—but fear I shall not be able to do it. I have no 'port folio.' My verses are scattered about on *scraps* of paper of all colours, shades, and degrees of antiquity. Uncle Phil has the only 'Book' I ever put them into, and that contains only my crudities—and only a few of *them*. More than what I have said, my papers generally in coming from Martinsburg to 'The Vineyard, near Millwood Clarke Co.' (Remember that as my

---

6. The *Broadway Journal,* II, No. 25 (December 27, 1845), 391. It is an interesting fact that nearly four years earlier, while Poe was connected with *Graham's Magazine,* he had included Cooke in his second "Chapter on Autography," published in that periodical, XIX, No. 6 (December, 1841). The entry reads: "P. P. Cooke, Esq., of Winchester, Va., is well known, especially in the South, as the author of numerous excellent contributions to the 'Southern Literary Messenger.' He has written some of the finest poetry of which America can boast. A little piece of his, entitled 'Florence Vane,' and contributed to the 'Gentleman's Magazine' of this city, during our editorship of that journal, was remarkable for the high ideality it evinced, and for the great delicacy and melody of its rhythm. It was universally admired and copied, as well here as in England. We saw it not long ago, *as original,* in Bentley's Miscellany! Mr. Cooke has, we believe, nearly ready for press, a novel called 'Maurice Werterbern,' whose success we predict with confidence. His MS. is clear, forcible, and legible, but disfigured by some little of that affectation which is scarcely a blemish in his literary style."

directive) caught on fire, not from their impetuosity of nature, but from the miserable Winchester and Potomac Engine, and were some quite, and most in part, *burnt*. Caleb Balderstone's fire and that of the Treasury Building will give you an idea of the benefit this gives me in excusing myself to my friends for the procrastinations and non performances of the last (how many!) years of my useless, but considerably happy life.

"I have been engaged for some months in writing a book of long poems called 'Froissart Ballads.' I have finished the 'Bridge of Lusac,' (the story of the Death of Sir John Chandos) and 'The Master of Bolton' and have opened a treaty (indirectly) with the Harpers[7] for the publication of it, a novel, a history of Virgin[ia] or a School Book or anything that will give me a few hundred per annum in addition to my present sufficient, but not super-abundant, means of living. I want a little 'Springs' and 'travel' money. These long poems, of course, would not suit Mr. Griswold. Of short ones it will take me a day or two to select and arrange such as I would not be ashamed to see printed. This requisite day or two, with the country delays of mail, will put it past the 8th before they could get to you—probably. I will however do my best to have them ready with the 'Biography'! If I can't, what shall I do?—Send them to Griswold (that would not look well—as he has not written to *me*) or keep them till your return? Write to me as soon as you get this, if you please, and say what I shall do.

"You say 'Give the Turkeys a holiday.' I got your letter in the midst of a party of my friends who were met here to eat a young gobler that I killed yesterday. I will however let his companions alone until I get rid of this task of 'fame and honour' that your cajolery of Griswold has put upon me. Write if you please at once."[8]

7. Nothing came of the "treaty," and no other mention of it has been found.
8. Kennedy Collection. Letter dated October 3, 1845.

Encouraged by his inclusion in Griswold's anthology, and perhaps by the interest Kennedy had revealed, Cooke sought advice from the latter regarding a literary career. He was just in a position to write, in Clarke County, and intended to combine the calling of an author with his other employments and amusements there. His domestic comforts were ample and, what was better, perfectly sure; but he wanted three or four hundred dollars per annum for "the usual trimmings," and this sum, probably, Kennedy could tell him how to make with his pen. Books, unless they caught the popular taste at a turn or by chance, did not bring money, he supposed; besides, publishers were hard to be got. It was somewhat beneath his dignity to contribute to most of the periodicals for money. Some of them, however, he believed, paid well and employed gentlemen and distinguished writers. He would be grateful if Kennedy would tell him something about such things, and put him in the way of becoming an established author.[9]

Kennedy's advice evidently included publication of a volume of verse, for on December 19 Cooke wrote: "I received your letter . . . and have been engaged ever since upon my French ballads. It has only today occurred to me that I might as well let you know that I received your letter and am busied in preparing my verses for you." The poetic mood, however, was a queer, capricious thing, and "the animal life I lead" was very apt, day after day, to banish it; consequently, the poems might not be ready for six weeks. It was important that his poetry should be finished, to the utmost degree, in his first grave adventure before the public;

---

9. Kennedy Collection. Letter dated November 15, 1845. In the same letter is illustrated the gulf between Cooke's country-gentleman notions regarding the ways of established authors and publishers, and the actuality. Only a month earlier he had sent materials to Griswold. Not having heard from the latter "or any other quarter," whether they were on time, "probably you have seen the new edition of his book," he suggested to Kennedy, "and can tell whether they are in it."

otherwise it would be easy to scribble any requisite quantity.¹⁰

While Cooke was being taken into the company of Griswold's poets and, spurred by Kennedy, was setting seriously to work at composition, he was also resuming the long-interrupted correspondence with Poe. So early as July 2, 1844, Poe had mentioned Cooke in a letter to James Russell Lowell. He, himself, Poe acknowledged, suffered from the constitutional indolence of which Lowell had complained. "Excessively slothful and wonderfully industrious—by fits," for him there were epochs when any kind of mental exercise was torture, when nothing yielded pleasure but solitary communion with the mountains and the woods. "I have thus rambled and dreamed away whole months, and awake, at last, to a sort of mania for composition. . . . This is also the temperament of P. P. Cooke of Va., the author of 'Florence Vane,' 'Young Rosalie Lee' and some other sweet poems—and I should not be surprised if it were your own. Cooke writes and thinks as you—and I have been told that you resemble him personally."¹¹

Late in 1845, Cooke had called on Poe for aid in the projected schemes of authorship he had also mentioned to Kennedy. Whatever Poe's advice—the letter has not been preserved—Cooke received from Poe the following April a message which, four months later, elicited this characteristic answer:

"MY DEAR SIR,—Your letter of Apr. 16th is to this day unanswered! I have however the excuse to make that I have been a good deal away from home, and whilst at home greatly drawn off from literature and its adjuncts by business, social interruptions, &c. This much of explanation, no

---
10. Kennedy Collection. Letter dated December 19, 1845. Kennedy's letters to Cooke in this connection have not been preserved.
11. Harvard University Library. Letter dated July 2, 1844.

doubt, will satisfy one so well assured as you must be of my regard and admiration.

"You propose that I shall take up your memoir where Lowell drops it, and carry it on to the present date of your publications. I will do so, if my long delay has not thrown the work into the hands of some other friend, with entire pleasure. I, however, have not Graham's Mag. for February, 1845, and if you still wish me to continue the memoir you must send that number to me. I some months ago procured your Tales and Poems, and have read them collectively with great pleasure. That is a wonderful poem ending—

> 'Hell rising from a thousand thrones
> Shall do it reverence.'

'Lenore,' too, is a great poem. The closing stanza of 'To one in Paradise' (I remember it as published in 'The Visionary') is the perfection of melody. 'The Raven' is your *best* poem.

"John Kennedy, talking with me about your stories, old and recent, said, 'the man's imagination is as truth-like and minutely accurate as De Foe's'—and went on to talk of your 'Descent into the Maelstrom,' 'MS. Found in a Bottle,' 'Gold Bug,' &c. I think this last the most ingenious thing I ever read. Those stories of criminal detection, 'Murders of the Rue Morgue,' &c., a prosecuting attorney in the neighborhood here declares are miraculous. I think your French friend, for the most part, fine in his deductions from over-laid and unnoticed small facts, but sometimes too minute and hair-splitting. The stories are certainly as interesting as any ever written. The 'Valdemar Case' I read in a number of your Broadway Journal last winter—as I lay in a Turkey blind, muffled to the eyes in overcoats, &c., and pronounce it without hesitation the most damnable, vraisemblable, horrible, hair-lifting, shocking, ingenious chapter of fiction that any brain ever conceived, or hands traced. That gelatinous, viscous sound of man's voice! there never was such an idea before. That story scared me in broad day, armed with a double-barrel Tryon Turkey gun. What would it have done at midnight in some old ghostly country-house?

"I have always found some one remarkable thing in your stories to haunt me long after reading them. The *teeth* in Berenice—the changing eyes of Morella—that red and glaring crack in the House of Usher—the pores of the deck in the MS. Found in a Bottle—the visible drops falling into the goblet in Ligeia, &c. &c.—there is always something of this sort to stick by the mind—by mine at least.

"My wife is about to enter the carriage and as I wish to send this to the P. O. by her, I must wind up rapidly. I *am now* after an interval of months again at work in the preparation of my poems for publication. I am *dragging,* but perhaps the mood will presently come. I bespeak a review of my Book at your hands when I get it out. I have not time now to copy Rosalie Lee. It is in Griswold's last edition. I am grateful to you for the literary prop you afford me; and trust to do something to justify your commendations. I talked recently with a little Lady who has heard a lecture of yours in which you praise my poetry—in New York. She had taken up the notion that I was a great poetic roaring Lion.

"Do with my MS. as you choose. What do you design as to the Stylus? Write to me without delay, if you can rob yourself of so much time."[12]

Poe's reply, five days later, gracefully accepted Cooke's apology for the delay in writing and thanked him "for the compliment":

---

12. Griswold Collection. Letter dated Millwood, August 4, 1846. The signature has been torn off. The letter and Poe's answer are either included or mentioned in most of the longer studies of Poe's life.

"Were I in a serious humor just now, I would tell you frankly how your words of appreciation make my nerves thrill—not because you praise me (for others have praised me more lavishly) but because I feel that you comprehend and discriminate. You are right about the hair-splitting of my French friend:—that is all done for effect. . . .

"Not for the world would I have had any one else to continue Lowell's Memoir until I have heard from you. I wish *you* to do it (if you will be so kind) and nobody else. By the time the book appears you will be famous, (or all my prophecy goes for nothing) and I shall have the *eclat* of your name to aid my sales. But, seriously, I do not think that any one so well enters into the poetical portion of my mind as yourself—and I deduce this idea from my intense appreciation of those points of your own poetry which seem lost upon others. . . .

"Griswold's new edition I have not yet seen (is it out?) but I will manage to find 'Rosalie Lee.' Do not forget to send me a few personal details of yourself—such as I give in 'The N. Y. Literati.' When your book appears I propose to review it fully in Colton's 'American Review.' If you ever write to him, please suggest to him that I wish to do so. I hope to get your volume before mine goes to press—so that I may speak more fully. . . ."[13]

As his letter to Poe suggests, Cooke had not wholly neglected for literature the avocations of a country gentleman. Too, there might be occasional business in the courts; and certainly there was the garden. "I am busy with hot-beds, gardening," he informed his father in March, 1846; but, also busy with composition, he added: "I think I am writing

---

13. From James A. Harrison, *Life and Letters of Edgar Allan Poe*, pp. 265-268. Cooke's "continuation" of Lowell's memoir appeared under the title "Edgar A. Poe" in the *Southern Literary Messenger*, XIV, 34-38 (January, 1848). Poe's proposal to review *Froissart Ballads* was not carried out, nor did Cooke appear among the "Literati."

some stirring poetry in my Froissart Ballads. The world shall decide before long."[14]

Not, however, until late in the year could Cooke announce to Kennedy that his poems were at last ready for publication. What, he inquired, was the next step? He was as ignorant as a child of all modes of approaching, or dealing with, publishers; and naturally leaned upon himself and Mr. Griswold. Mr. G. had written to him last spring that he would gladly give his services with the publishing houses. He had dedicated the volume to Kennedy, as he was the literary head of the Pendleton clan. For himself, he thought the poems artistical and readable. "The Froissart ballads are five in number, and about a dozen miscellaneous poems accompany them—whole bulk about 130 printed pages." A postscript added:

"I will write by this same mail to Griswold in Philadelphia, letting him know that you have the control of my finished MSS. and requesting his advice and assistance. Poe is ready to puff me at the North, and Minor's Messenger open to my friends here. Judge B. Tucker of Williamsburg or J. P. Heath of Richmond will fill my sails for the South—*if a publisher will launch me.* If this literary enterprise fails the devil take pen and paper henceforth."[15]

In a message to Griswold, Cooke largely repeated what had been said to Kennedy. He was quite as ignorant as any country gentleman ever was of the business part of literature, and "no doubt if my ballads are not to be printed until I (personally) induce a publisher to print them, they

14. Cooke Collection. Letter dated March 15, 1846. The letter closed with this postscript: "Please send Minor the 2d. Broadway Journal with Poe's notice of my poem—black-lined to draw his attention to it. I have had so many applications for the poem (copies of it) that I wish it printed speedily. Poe's puff, reprinted, would give wings to it. Thousands think according to critical decision."—In the May number of the *Southern Literary Messenger* Minor published "The Mountains," the poem to which Cooke evidently referred.

15. Kennedy Collection. Letter dated November 8, 1846.

will be converted into gun wads first." Poe held himself ready to review the book; Tucker or Heath would doubtless "stand God-father to me here and in the South. So that if there is any spark in my poems it will not be left to die out for want of blowing—puffing perhaps would be the better word."[16]

Neither Kennedy nor Griswold having answered, Cooke two weeks later sent the manuscript on to Baltimore, where with an accompanying letter[17] it reached Kennedy just after the latter had composed a message of advice. At Griswold's suggestion, Cooke learned, Cooke was to put the whole of his songs and tales into Griswold's hands—"by the by, it is a *devilish* way of using a man, that—and let him *deal* them out to Graham who would be glad to give you some twenty-five or fifty dollars for a few pages each month." Afterward, they would appear in a volume, which Griswold thought would be more saleable for Graham's "heralding." The suggestion struck Kennedy as a good one, and he therefore commended it to Cooke's notice.[18] The suggestion also struck Cooke as a good one, and he wrote immediately to both mentors, leaving the matter wholly to their joint control.[19]

The poems were not, however, to profit by Graham's heralding, perhaps for a reason Cooke, himself, had foreseen. To Griswold, in a letter which, composed by a character less forthright than Cooke's, would have seemed disingenuous, he had remarked: "The serious drawback to the

---

16. Griswold Collection. Letter dated November 8, 1846.

17. Kennedy Collection. Letter dated November 23, 1846. It contained this interesting passage: "I regard the poems sent as on the whole, not much—but narrative poetry, if at all dramatic, and not too fine, or too much on magnificent stilts, is readable—generally; and the public may find mine so."

18. Kennedy Collection. Letter from Kennedy to Cooke, dated November 26, 1846.

19. Griswold Collection, Cooke to Griswold, letter dated November 26, 1846; Kennedy Collection, Cooke to Kennedy, letter dated November 27, 1846.

The Vineyard and "Froissart Ballads" 77

publication of the poems in Graham is the fact that the *best* of them contains about 1500 lines—rather a long 'Ballad.'" Of the five ballads in all, three were "about as long as the Proem (published by you in your Poets)—the remaining ones quite short." Doubtless Griswold had formed some idea that they were like Lockhart's Spanish Ballads, in length; if they were they would have suited better for magazine publication. As for the quality of the poems, he would not forestall Griswold's critical judgment by saying that he thought them bad; "but, rest assured, I shall do better things hereafter."[20]

Griswold evidently thought well of the ballads, and through his efforts a publisher was found. Carey and Hart, a Philadelphia firm of high repute, would accept the volume, Cooke was informed. He wrote thanking Griswold for the compliment of "your approbation of my verses," but criticizing his own work. The ballads were certainly not in the high key of a man warm with his subject, and doing the thing finely; "I wrote them with the reluctance of a turkey hunter kept from his sport." Only Mr. Kennedy's urgent entreaty and remonstrance had whipped him up to the labor. This year, however, he would fan the fires, and make a rush for fame:

20. Griswold Collection. Letter dated November 26, 1846. In his sketch of Cooke in the *International,* Griswold quoted from another letter which contained criticism of the ballads by their author. The excerpt is given here; all efforts to discover the original have failed:

"You will find them beneath your sanguine prognostic. They are mere narrative poems, designed for the crowd. Poetic speculation, bold inroads upon the debateable land—'the wild weird clime, out of space out of time'—I have not here attempted. I *will* hereafter merge myself in the nobler atmosphere; in the meantime I have stuck to the ordinary level, and have endeavored to write interesting stories in verse, with grace and spirit. I repeat my fear that in writing for the cold, I have failed to touch the quick and warm—in writing for a dozen hunting companions, who have been in the habit of making my verse a *post prandium* entertainment, and never endured an audacity of thought or word, I have tamed myself out of your approbation." "Philip Pendleton Cooke," *The International Magazine,* IV (October, 1851), 302.

"Will you have the kindness to put as a note to the mention of Actaeon in the ballad 'Sir Peter of Bearn' the following, or something like it.

" 'Shakespeare, and the old writers generally, Lord Berners amongst the rest, spell Actaeon as I have done above; the delay on the dipthong, in pronunciation, is discordant in verse of rapid measure, and for that reason I have retained the ancient English spelling.'

"This note you may not deem necessary; but I dread an inelegance. Add it or not as you think best. If Mr. Graham publishes any of the poetry do not be too exacting as to price. Tell him to send me his magazine—if he publishes them."[21]

Ten days later, Griswold having warned him regarding the meagerness of the literary fruits that might be expected by an as yet little-known author, Cooke hastened to answer his advisor. He had given Griswold, he recalled, full power to contract with the publishers, and would not have hesitated an instant to sanction his *giving* them the work. Of course, therefore, the offer of ten per cent by Carey and Hart was accepted. Indeed, he was somewhat mortified that his limited means and family obligations made it impossible to issue the book at his own charge:

"I am not surprised at what you say concerning Graham and Godey. Whatever may be my literary rank hereafter, I am yet in obscurity, and magazine articles derive nine-tenths of their pecuniary value to publishers from the known and famous names attached to them. Longfellow's worst poem, however a best chance effort of mine might excel it, would be vastly more valuable to Graham than anything I could send him. Before hearing of the prize-poem mode of getting supplies, these were my views on the subject, and I expected very little from the magazines—pecuniarily...."[22]

21. Griswold Collection. Letter dated January 20, 1847.
22. Griswold Collection. Letter dated February 1, 1847. Griswold's letter, to which the foregoing is in answer, apparently has not been preserved.

Notwithstanding the relative obscurity of Cooke, *Graham's* had printed during 1846 three of his poems—for which, however, there is no evidence that the author ever received payment. "Emily" had appeared in January; "To My Daughter Lily," in August; "Lines," in September. In its June number the *American Review* had reprinted "The Power of the Bards"; and in September the *Western Centinel* of Baltimore had given further currency to "To My Daughter Lily." If still obscure as compared with Longfellow, Cooke was no longer unknown outside Virginia and the South.

The bulk, however, of his new work during the year, apart from the ballads, had appeared in the *Southern Literary Messenger*. To the April number he had contributed "Old Books and New Authors," a discerning essay which, occasioned by a reference by Poe to one of Cooke's poems,[23] discussed conscious and unconscious plagiarism in both poetry and prose and cited examples in Poe's own work. A long narrative poem, "The Murder of Cornstalk," appeared in the June number, and the sentimental "Love and Be Kind" in July. Under the title "Dante," the September number carried a critical review of Cary's translation of *The Divina Commedia;* and appended to the review appeared "The Famine Tower," Cooke's poetic version of the story of Ugolino as translated by Cary. Altogether, if the ballads be included, Cooke had composed during 1846 a respectable volume of verse and prose; and, looking back at the close of the year, he might well have congratulated himself that the man of literature had made progress in disciplining the turkey hunter.

Publication of *Froissart Ballads* gave Cooke a measure of self-confidence and cautious hope which the appearance of his verse in periodicals had hardly been adequate to arouse.

---

23. "Emily."

"My literary life opens now," he wrote to Griswold. "If the world manifest any disposition to hear my 'utterances' it will be abundantly gratified. I am 30; until 40 letters shall be my mind's calling—avoiding however to rely on them pecuniarily—then (after 40) politics will be a sequitur."[24]

The reception accorded his volume when it appeared on the reviewers' desks justified, on the whole, Cooke's optimism. The *National Intelligencer* gave to its discussion almost two columns of space, in which the ballads were spoken of as "an advantageous specimen of that sort of American composition to which they belong—if, indeed, there have been any other like attempts, in this country, deserving serious mention."[25] The *Literary World* hailed the volume warmly, and also at length, for "If anything in literature can properly be termed refreshing, it certainly is an American book which appeals, naturally and honestly, to that taste for the romantic which used to be supposed inherent in cultivated and generous minds, but which has been wellnigh extinguished under the conventional, the analytic, the utilitarian tendency of our age and country."[26] As for the *Knickerbocker* critic, while certain stanzas seemed to be lacking in harmony, yet the ballads as a whole had stood well the "severe test of comparison" with "those glorious lays of Macaulay," which for the twentieth time the critic had, he informed, just read.[27]

"This is one of the most delightful volumes which we have met with for many a day," declared the reviewer for

24. Griswold Collection. Letter dated February 19, 1847. "You are probably right in your preference for the Proem," Cooke added. "It was written with excessive care. The Master of Bolton was written not so lingeringly but still quite slowly. Orthone et id omne genus were dashed off with as much rapidity as I write this—altho', of course, slowly revised and pruned afterward. The Story of Ugolino I think the best thing in the book."
25. The *Daily National Intelligencer*, Washington, D. C. (March 18, 1847).
26. *Literary World*, I (March 27, 1847), 173-75.
27. *Knickerbocker Magazine*, XXIX (April, 1847), 366.

The Vineyard and "Froissart Ballads"

Graham's, adding: "We have long known and admired the fugitive poems of Mr. Cooke, and now heartily welcome our old favorites, with their new companions, in the beautiful dress which the publishers have given them."[28] And by the *Southern Literary Messenger* it was welcomed as "a charming little volume ... the harbinger of better things."[29]

Cooke's own commentary on the ballad poems, expressed at greater length than in his correspondence with Griswold and Kennedy, fortunately has been preserved in a letter which also provides information regarding his theory of poetry. Late in March, 1847, he replied to a communication from Beverley Tucker:

"Your letter of the 20th I received yesterday and lose no time in answering it. What you say about the modern taste for discords in measure, is doubtless true enough; but I think of some qualifications of your opinion, which I have not time now to write down. As regards the changes in your speech of Viola,[30] I felt no disposition to change what I saw no occasion for changing, but did what you requested, leaving to your judgment, to make a right choice between the original and the new. Such trivial changes are the mere varieties of wording with which literary men toy and amuse themselves. The only secret that I know for making poetic measure sound rough without becoming unmusical, is to violate the right placing of an accent here and there, and to terminate the line with a word of two or more syllables where the accent is on the penultimate syllable, leaving the ultimate a metrical superfluity.

"'That he for whom I bore this degrada-tion'—is an instance of this last. It was in accordance with my notion

---

28. *Graham's Magazine,* XXX (May, 1847), 323-324.
29. *Southern Literary Messenger,* XIII (July, 1847), 437-439. The review was from the hand of Beverley Tucker. Authorship of the other reviews cannot be determined, though the phrasing of *Graham's* reviewer suggests Griswold's style.
30. Character in Tucker's poetic drama of that name.

of shifting accents to produce discord, that I introduced '*hav*ing no consolation' and '*feed*ing my mind,' instead of 'and *find* no consolation' and 'and *feed* my mind.' The changes are altogether slight and trivial, and wholly unworthy to be thought of in reference to the real grave merit of the passage."

Cooke feared very much that Tucker had been disappointed in his book of poems. The criticism Tucker had given on "Tetenoire" was entirely just; in fact: "I never was satisfied with the *tone* of that poem, and now you let me into the secret reason of my dislike of it. I have told an old ballad tale in the manner of the pretty, thought-diluting, modern school of versifiers.... I dashed off a prose sentence containing the rapid outline of the story, with some honest old ballad feeling in my blood at the time, but wrote it many months afterwards in the hurry of completing my book for print, and when all feeling of the sort was gone.

"Orthone (which my dear wife who is staunch for Geoffrey cannot bear on account of the 'sow') is, I think, vastly better, because it is *true to the Froissart tone*. Even the homely 'devilment' of the straw and the sow, I think would have been badly exchanged for more graceful apparitions of the merry spirit in the shapes of a singing bird, and stag; shapes which I had half an idea of violating Froissart so far as to make him assume. I recollected in time, the difference between the northern and southern genius of Europe, and retained the rude Gothic images of the north, where Froissart had put them. Sir Peter of Bearn is also passable in tone, but wants *point* of event, in the end. Read my preface and that 'deputy preface' just before Orthone, in connection with these poems.

"The lines you quote from the ancient ballad are great—greater doubtless than the old bard took them to be.

'The king looked over his left shoulder—
A grim look looked he.'

The *picture* here, of the fierce old man, is as clear as noonday. I dwarf before that ancient power of words. But is not the world of readers to blame for a great part of the modern incompetency? They would not tolerate that rude brevity of utterance, or would forget to take in the vivid picture because not more ostentatiously 'done up.'

"The Master of Bolton and the miscellaneous poems will better please you doubtless than the other 'Ballads.' A word as to the name *Ballads*. My poems were *designed* to be ballads, after the manner of Lockhart's Spanish ones. The proem was printed *as* a 'proem to the Froissart Ballads.' I was committed in print to the name. I wrote all of them after the proem, and they assumed a shape and look very different from the original design, and are, in fact, only *ballads*, by courtesy of the most liberal interpretation of the word—as Scott's poem of Branksome was a *Lay*...."

As for Cooke's influence and acquaintance with booksellers and managers of theaters, which Tucker evidently had solicited, he had none. This recent book of his was his first. Carey and Hart bought it of him through Griswold and John Kennedy, who had spurred him to the task of writing it with six months' praise and growling at his idleness. Whatever it might gain him in the shape of acquaintance or influence with publishers, of course would be at Tucker's service.[31]

Apparently it was to gain for Cooke nothing more valuable than acquaintance, notwithstanding the critics' praise and the real merits of the book as a first performance. Fifteen months after its publication he had received no royalty,[32] nor is there any proof that he ever did. True, shortly

---

31. From P. W. Turrentine's copy of the original in the Coleman Manuscript Collection. Letter dated March 29, 1847.

32. "The copyright has never been credited nor amt paid 10c—750 copies/HhB."—Notation on a letter of inquiry from Cooke to Carey and Hart, dated July 27, 1848, in the Ford Collection, New York Public Library.

after the death of Cooke, Griswold indicated otherwise to John R. Thompson, then editor of the *Messenger:*

"So P. P. Cooke—the finest poet that ever lived in Virginia—one of the finest that have written in our days—is dead. I corresponded with him for years, and made the arrangements for bringing out his Poems, in Philad'a—obtaining, to his surprise, I believe a hundred dollars of copy-money. I read all his proofs, too—and the while had hopes of the 'Ballads' creating a sensation—which they did not. Can not something be done for his widow, with his MSS. and uncollected poems and prose writings that are in print? If you will undertake the preparation of his works, I will do all I can do in the matter of printing them and making them profitable. You certainly did not exaggerate his merits in the *Messenger.*"[33] There is, however, no evidence of the payment of copy money except Griswold's memory. Judged by material rewards, the career of Virginia's "finest poet" must be regarded as a failure.

It was not, however, a failure judged by other standards. True, the quantity of Cooke's published verse is less than that of most poets who claim title to literary recognition; and none of it is poetry of the highest order. Of the thirty-eight extant poems, totaling about five thousand lines, that can be identified as his, Cooke, himself, rejected for publication in his volume most of the early ones as being either too sentimental in mood or too imitative in manner. But some twenty-five of the poems, containing four fifths of the lines, possess considerable merit. This merit derives partly from Cooke's narrative skill, partly from his style, partly from his ability to recreate in imagination and to set forth

33. The University of Virginia library. Letter dated February 19, 1850. Thompson evidently did not act on the suggestion but may have communicated it to John Esten Cooke, who later corresponded with Griswold regarding the subject. For details see Griswold Collection, letter, John Esten Cooke to Rufus W. Griswold, dated Richmond, February 3, 1851.

characters, scenes, and incidents of long ago. To these must be added, with reference to the lyrical poems, his ability to convey simply and directly the emotional values of his own experience.

Of these four qualities, what is most distinctive and individual in Cooke's poetry is expressed in the second and the last. In the technique of verse narration, Cooke may have been schooled by Scott, whom he doubtless read closely, and by Chaucer, whom he had loved since his Princeton days. His fondness for medieval characters and settings, as instanced in "The Ballad of Count Herman," might have been stimulated not only by Froissart's narratives but by the poetry of Keats and Coleridge.[34] In his nature lyrics, too, there may be some reflection of Wordsworth the nature-lover, not the metaphysician. As a group, however, Cooke's lyrics are essentially non-derivative; they express gracefully the emotions of a genuine poet who was moved deeply by love, by the chivalrous virtues, and by the more striking aspects of nature.

Cooke's style, like his subject matter, may have owed something to other poets; but even more than his lyricism it seems distinctive, non-derivative. What it is, can be suggested by indicating what it is not. There is nothing in it of the verbal magic of a Coleridgean line. It has little of the sonorous music of Wordsworth's great odes. Of Shelley's or Byron's manner there seems to be no trace, and even less if possible, of Poe's. On the other hand, Cooke's developed style does bear a general resemblance to (without, of course,

---

34. It would be difficult to discover in the later poetry of Cooke evidence of specific influence by any of his contemporaries or immediate predecessors, either English or American. He read widely; he must have known the poetry of the Elder and Younger Romantics in England and of Bryant at home. Poe's poetry he also knew, and admired, though he has less to say about it than about Poe's tales. But no contemporary—least of all Poe, Cooke's friendship with whom might suggest a literary influence—seems to have been either a model for imitation or a source of direct inspiration.

ever equaling) that of the mature Keats. It has something of the same melodic grace and variety, the same easy directness of manner—it expresses a similarly deep and spontaneous poetic feeling disciplined, as was Keats's, by a classic sense of form. In addition, it possesses a verbal vigor that must be considered as a reflection of Cooke's own vigorous, out-door life in the hills and valleys of western Virginia.

Perhaps in geography, after all, is to be found the clue to what is of peculiar merit in Cooke's poetry, and to his failure to attain higher rank. As a poet Cooke had superior native endowment. His inclinations led him, as Keats had been led, more and more strongly to the past, when with his reading he became aware, like Keats, of the poetic riches that the past had accumulated for the uses of a poet's imagination. Like Keats, though less consciously and imposingly, he sought to create poetry in which medieval pageantry would be subdued by classic form. But there was no group of friends or critics in western Virginia interested in such efforts; and nowhere in America was there a considerable public willing to pay much attention to them should they succeed. Neglected as Keats was, he had far more to sustain his ambition than Virginia or America offered Cooke.

In a sense, then, environment defeated the poet Cooke, though it helps to account for a quality hardly found theretofore in American poetry. Had he lived in England, he might have achieved recognition as a fine poet whose work showed some affinities with that of Keats. Living in America, he gave up verse-making when the practical side of his mind told him that it added no butter to bread.

CHAPTER VI

Prose Works

DURING HIS few remaining years Cooke probably continued to write verse; but the scanty pay for a poet's wares had discouraged publication and turned his thoughts to the field of prose. Only one other poem, the rather artificial "Pan and Echo," appeared in print.[1] On the other hand, his published work in the field of prose was considerable, both in quantity and in quality.

A renewed interest in the critical essay, the form with which Cooke had experimented ten years earlier at Glengary, already had been evidenced by the publication in 1846 of "Old Books and New Authors" and "Dante." This interest continued, and during 1847 the rather formidable "Living Novelists" appeared in three installments in the *Messenger*. The general plan of the study is comparable to that of the earlier "English Poetry." It consists of a series of judgments and commentaries in logical arrangement—such an arrangement as a mind trained in and influenced by, even though disliking, the law might unconsciously choose. The judgments, however, are more keen and mature, and the style is more polished, than in the essays of Cooke's youth.

The same adjectives apply to "Edgar A. Poe" and to "The Feudal Armies of France and England," contributed to the

---

[1]. "The Gazelle," a parody of Poe's "The Raven" published in *The New York Mirror* for May 3, 1845, was credited by John H. Ingram to Cooke (*The Raven*, by Edgar Allan Poe, p. 94). Its author, however, was the art critic Clarence Chatham Cooke, not Philip Pendleton Cooke.

Messenger for January and June, 1848. The former, published under Cooke's signature, is the promised continuation of Lowell's memoir of Poe. It compares favorably with the work of Lowell; and, with the earlier "Old Books and New Authors," it is especially interesting for the proof it affords of the author's ability to make and willingness to express independent literary judgments. "The Feudal Armies of France and England," signed only with an initial but almost certainly contributed by Cooke, displays not only his passion for the romantic aspects of the age of chivalry but also his knowledge of its social classes and institutions. It displays, too, with the other essays a vigorous good sense which illuminated whatever object of criticism its author's mind examined.

Meritorious as the essays are, they reflect the lesser, not the major, talent of their author as a writer of prose; and they constitute the minor part of his published prose work. The bulk of that work appeared as a series of fictional contributions to the *Messenger* during the years 1848 and 1849 and in the early months of 1850. The contributions belong to two classes: sketches, and prose tales—tales suggestive, by their length, of the fiction form which later in the century was to develop as the novelette.

As the setting for the first of these tales, *John Carper, the Hunter of Lost River,* Cooke used frontier western Virginia during the Revolution. The characters, all of them frontier types, are individualized; and the plot, simple but well conceived and exciting, unfolds without the moralizing or needless mechanics which occasionally mar the work of Cooke's great predecessor, James Fenimore Cooper. In his treatment of the Indian, Cooke is more realistic than Cooper. The descriptive passages, especially those of the wilderness about the Blackwater River, perhaps equal in graphic power any of similar nature that had been written by an American author. The style is as direct, plain, and vigorous as the character of the hunter whose name gives the title of the tale.

The other novelettes, *The Two Country Houses, The Gregories of Hackwood,* and *The Crime of Andrew Blair,* have in common the fact that they deal in the main with the aristocratic society of the lower Shenandoah in which Cooke had spent the years of his youth and his maturity. They have, too, a looseness in plot and a certain easy ingenuity in invention not rare in the fiction of an era whose taste was still dominated by Scott and Dumas. But in excellence of style they are superior to most of the periodical fiction of the day, as well as in the power of the author to image scenes and situations and to recreate characters, whose originals he had doubtless often observed. Taken together, they give a detailed picture of western Virginia during the eighteen-thirties and forties, a picture which in most details, the reader will feel, was drawn from life.

Longest of all the novelettes, *The Two Country Houses* is the final form of the story which, years earlier, Cooke had planned to write and had given the title "Mary Hunter of Cotsworth." But though longest, it is not the best of his tales. It contains the least compact plot of the four. Its heroine is the least lifelike of all the women Cooke drew, and far less interesting than the flesh-and-blood Mary Evelina Hunter Dandridge, whom he probably had in mind when he first conceived the story. In her ladyhood she reflected too many of the virtues with which Scott and Cooper endowed their heroines. The hero, Carabas Car, is hardly more convincing. Cooke presents him as the impetuous, high-spirited, reckless Virginia Cavalier youth who, his oats having been sown, will then grow up to be the splendid husband of a pure and lovely maiden. His youthful extravagances, however, seem rather far-fetched even for a Virginia country gentleman;[2] and his ability suddenly to begin writing profound articles on international affairs for Paris newspapers—this, perhaps, as a reflex of disappointed love—violates the reader's sense of reality.

Most of the minor characters, however, some of whom are representative of a lower class then beginning to tread on the economic heels of an impoverished landed gentry, are drawn with fidelity to human nature. In the account of the wanderings of the hero, Cooke manages to present much realistic material apparently gathered during his own journey to Missouri. Moreover, the story excellently mirrors the decaying agrarian society of western Virginia before the War Between the States.

The Crime of Andrew Blair, which has been called "a study of a respectable planter with a criminal past,"[3] has a more concentrated plot than its predecessor and a more credible heroine, though it, too, exhibits some of the features of romantic fiction.

The story may be briefly summarized as follows: Andrew Blair, whose passions "are swift and dangerous, but rather those of a woman than masculine," is insulted by his guest, "blunt, frank, choleric" Colonel Arthur Pellew, who fancies that Blair has injured him. Blair follows Pellew, stabs him, and throws the body in a well. Jack Herries, boorish son of a haglike mother, is a chance witness of the deed. His knowledge of the crime gives Jack a hold on Andrew Blair, which he uses to advance his own fortunes. He marries; and a son and a daughter are born. He continues to amass lands and property. But over him hangs his debt to Andrew Blair, whose money has provided the lever for his rise to

2. It is possible, of course, that Cooke endowed his hero with the qualities of his own boyhood, an hypothesis to which his early exploits as a lover give some credence.

3. David K. Jackson, "Philip Pendleton Cooke: Virginia Gentleman, Lawyer, Hunter, and Poet," *American Studies in Honor of William Kenneth Boyd*, ed. by David Kelly Jackson, p. 319.

affluence and position; and he fears that the death of Blair, on whose heirs he would have no hold, might destroy the imposing edifice he has been able to erect through the years on the foundation of guilty knowledge. The solution is to marry his son to Miss Minny, Blair's niece and prospective heir.

Tom Herries is ugly, as the son of Jack Herries might well be expected to be, and he acts the part of a fool, also appropriately enough. But in him there are good qualities—doubtless the contribution of his mother, whose lineage is quite respectable. Moreover, he really loves Miss Minny. By his excellent horsemanship and by his readiness to die in a marvelous leap over a chasm, which strains belief, her contempt is transmuted into love. She nurses him through illness, draws him back to life and hope. The now aged Andrew Blair sickens, confesses his crime, dies; the others, including the time-softened John Herries, live thereafter in the happiness appropriate to romances.

So condensed, the story seems hardly probable; and the original contains passages which show that Cooke had not yet assimilated the influences of the various authors whose works he no doubt had studied—among them, the tales of Poe. He yet lacks the practical skill which makes for unity of tone, the refined sense of proportion which contents itself with the essential in motivation of action. To illustrate: In the otherwise sound plot, Cooke needs to supply a motive for Tom Herries' leap across the chasm. He provides it by having a minor character tell at the dinner table a long anecdote—a "tall tale"—which though excellent in itself is cumbersomely long for its function. But structurally, *The Crime of Andrew Blair* is a better story than *The Two Country Houses;* and it reveals a power of description more matured.

The Gregories of Hackwood is also structurally better,

more concentrated and direct. Miles Gregory, once an accomplished gentleman, possesses great wealth and three children, but is himself possessed by a consuming lust for gold. This lust prompts him to allow his estate to lie barren, to deny financial aid to his blind son, to make his two daughters ashamed and unhappy, and to begrudge his own body the bits of stale bread and cheese which keep life in it. For the younger daughter, Anne, the old man retains some paternal affection; but his miserliness stands between her and her lover, Henry Grant.

The elder daughter, high-spirited Joan, arranges a meeting between the miser and his unfortunate son; and a momentary flicker of a father's pity prompts the gift of a debtor's bond whose value, though dubious, seems to promise relief to the son from the degradation of abject poverty. But the old man's cupidity is played on by a shrewd lawyer, whose clients offer to redeem the bond for half its face value. In a painful scene the miser demands the return of the paper and leaves daughter, son, and the latter's helpless family in utter despair. That night, moved by fear for the safety of his hoard, which Joan had threatened to rob if need be in order to aid her brother, the miser attempts to hide it away in an abandoned quarry. But as, weighted with his burden, he crosses a stream swollen by a storm, the hand-rail gives and he falls in, to drown beneath his gold.

The solution to the problems created by the miser's adamantine vice is now easy. The son's eyesight is restored by expert medical care. The two lovers marry and make the old estate once more bloom as of old. Joan, preyed on for a time by the thought that her threats had caused the father's death, at last "regained the spring of her bold nature, and came to look upon life more hopefully . . . she became the wife of an honorable and distinguished man, of great force of character, and lives now in a distant country."[4]

4. *Messenger*, XIV (October, 1848), 622.

The story has much more artistry than its plot, thus condensed, and its easy ending would suggest. Both sisters are more convincing than Mary Hunter; the miser is drawn with graphic power; and the wily lawyer is presented with all the relish Cooke had earlier displayed in his characterization of the money-lender and his ungainly son in *The Two Country Houses*. Cooke's excellent gift for dialogue is employed to best advantage. Throughout the story are passages, such as those describing the storm and the discovery of the miser's body, which reveal the author's capacity to convey in a few strokes and without apparent art the essential quality of a person or a scene.

The three fictional sketches composed by Cooke during his last years are much shorter than the novelettes, and their value is slighter. "Captain Guy; or, The Unpardonable Sin," interesting as further revealing Cooke's fondness for Froissart and medieval themes, also displays his resourcefulness in dialogue; mainly by this means are the characters of the sacrilegious captain of the Free Companions, his ruffian henchmen, and the craven abbot portrayed. "Joseph Jenkins' Researches Into Antiquity: Erisicthon" affords Cooke opportunity for a breezy, sophisticated burlesque of the fable of Erysicthon as related by Ovid. Also a burlesque—or, rather, a satire—is the posthumously published dialogue sketch "A Morning with Cagliostro. From Notes of a Conversation with Mr. Joseph Jenkins," which through deft imitation and portrayal of Dumas good-naturedly holds that prodigious author up to ridicule.

Also published after Cooke's death was "The Turkey-hunter in the Closet," probably written to serve as the first chapter of a projected book dealing with the author's experiences as a hunter and sportsman in the Shenandoah Valley. It contains a rambling essay on hunting, followed by a humorous account of Cooke's first turkey hunt; and it vividly paints scenes of Cooke's youth in the merry society of Winchester.

The unfinished prose romance, *The Chevalier Merlin*, which contains the best of his prose fiction, is a prophecy of what Cooke might have become had not his life, like the history of his hero, been cut off in mid career. Here his style, graphic, fluent, seemingly artless in its strength and informality, has achieved full maturity. Here, too, his characters seem most surely and consistently pictured, his settings most deftly sketched.

Some suggestion of the nature of the novel is contained in John Esten Cooke's *Messenger* sketch of his brother. Referring to "a letter before us," which apparently is no longer extant, he quotes the author's description of *The Chevalier Merlin* as being a novel, "which starting from a Norse hill reaches to Bender, and back again to Gothland. The Chevalier is with Charles XII at Bender. I made the story in a few hours."[5] But this fragmentary quotation gives only a general impression of a work which, in so far as it was completed, is as rich in color and incident as any of Scott's novels. A somewhat more illuminating statement regarding the historical aspects of the story, also from the pen of its author, is prefixed to the first chapter:

"Merlin Brand, a Norwegian, entered the service of Charles the Twelfth of Sweden a short time before the battle of Pultowa, and remained with his royal master quite to the end of the mad comedy of Bender. He saw the czar Peter, he came in contact with the rival kings of Poland, he traversed the parched plains between the Boristhenes and Otzacow with Mazeppa the Hetman, he witnessed the state of three viziers, and the muster of Turkish armies on the beautiful levels of Adrianople, he was brought into daily intercourse with brave and distinguished gentlemen of many

5. "Recollections," *Messenger*, XXVI (June, 1858), 428.

countries, he was much about the person of the king his master and read the nature of that most remarkable of the monarchs of the time closely: some chapters of his life, therefore, cannot fail to interest the reader, if they are written with even a small degree of skill. Apart from these adjuncts of a higher and more widely interesting character, his private adventures were not wanting in romantic incident. With so much of prologue, I begin my narrative of some passages in the life of the Chevalier Merlin."[6]

Even Cooke's prologue, however, scarcely suggests the variety of the chevalier's private adventures or the multiplicity of the characters whom Merlin encountered. The story, unfinished though it is, is too long for summary here. It must suffice to say that, in its historical aspects, the plot follows closely Voltaire's account of the career of Charles XII; in its wealth of invention, its masterful portrayal of character, its freshness and vigor of style, *The Chevalier Merlin* compares favorably with the best of the historical romances of its day.

How Cooke would have concluded the adventures of his hero—there remained to be resolved a misunderstanding with a pride-wounded damsel back in Sweden, and a deadly feud with her cousin—must remain a matter of inference. He wrote rapidly when in the humor to write; but apparently, the humor came only just in time to enable him to meet the *Messenger's* deadline for copy.[7] Moreover, he wrote, it would seem, without preliminary sketching of

6. *Messenger*, XV (June, 1849), 326. The story was published serially beginning with the June, 1849, number and running consecutively through the number for January, 1850, with the exception of the number for October, which contained no installment. The seven installments comprise twenty chapters. Beginning with the third installment, the material was copyrighted in the editor's name, doubtless (no reason is given) to protect a work likely to be pirated.

7. Chapters XVII-XXI, the last installment, published in the January, 1850, number, were not yet prepared early in the preceding December. See a letter from Cooke to his father, dated November 29, 1849, in the Cooke Collection.

plot; and although the manuscript of the final installment has been preserved, no other document from Cooke's pen remains to indicate his intentions with respect to the chevalier. In view of the tendencies exhibited in his other fiction, however, it must be inferred that Cooke would have had Merlin at last regain the heroine's affections. An account of the death of Charles XII might, too, have been expected.

By the few commentators whose criticism of *The Chevalier Merlin* has been recorded, the work has been uniformly praised. John R. Thompson, then editor of the *Southern Literary Messenger,* spoke of it as "the singularly beautiful story of the fortunes of Charles XII" and went on to quote in his notice of the death of Cooke a far abler critic than himself: "The late Edgar A. Poe expressed himself to us in terms of the warmest eulogy of the first three parts of this remarkable production, which he declared to be without a counterpart in American letters."[8] Griswold also, it would seem, thought highly of the tale and supposed that it might be published, as John Esten desired, in book form.[9] Finally, Mott in his history of American periodicals notes that although the serials in the *Messenger* "were often quite unimportant," an exception "may be made in behalf of P. P. Cooke's 'Chevalier Merlin.'"[10]

Comparison of the fiction and the poetry of Cooke reveals

8. "Editor's Table," *Messenger,* XVI (February, 1850), 126. John Esten Cooke, in an unpublished sketch of his brother, has the following: "Edgar A. Poe declared in the hearing of the writer of this sketch that *The Chevalier Merlin* was less a novel than a poem and that no one but Mr. Cooke could have written it." The sketch is in the possession of John Esten's son, Dr. R. P. Cooke, of Lexington, Va.

9. "That 'Merlin' should appear in volume form no one can doubt—in the style for example of Longfellow's 'Kavanagh'—for like that book it is rather a prose-poem than a carelessly written tale. . . ." From a letter from John Esten Cooke to Griswold, dated February 3, 1851, in the Griswold Collection. The letter indicates Griswold's opinion, previously expressed.

10. Frank Luther Mott, *A History of American Magazines,* p. 650. The remaining references to the work merely echo the criticisms of Thompson, Griswold, or Poe.

a significant parallelism in choice of subject matter. It suggests, too, that his creative talent was less at ease in the present than in the past. His first prose tale, *John Carper,* dealt with the general theme of frontier life in Colonial times. So did two of the early poems, "The Song of the Sioux Lovers" and "The Last Indian," though, it is true, less successfully than the prose work or the later poem "The Murder of Cornstalk." *The Two Country Houses, The Gregories of Hackwood,* and *The Crime of Andrew Blair,* which may be taken to represent a second stage in the development of Cooke as a fiction writer, employed themes and materials appropriate to western Virginia in his day, and may well have been inspired in part by personal observation and experience. Similarly, the poems "Life in the Autumn Woods" and "The Mountains," transitional in the poetry, reflected firsthand knowledge of nature in contemporary western Virginia.

In the third stage of his development both as a poet and as a novelist, Cooke turned away from Virginia to find subject matter in the glamorous past, his fondness for which had been cultivated fifteen years earlier in the library of Princeton University. Inspiration for his best narrative poetry—at any rate, for his best ballad poetry—derived from the pages of Froissart; and if he added freely to what he found there, as, for example, in "The Master of Bolton," his longest poem, he did so with the sure touch of a talent that has mastered itself and its materials. *The Chevalier Merlin,* Cooke's longest and best prose tale, is likewise unrelated to Virginia, as little concerned as the poetry with life there or, for that matter, life anywhere in the United States.

One might infer from such facts that Cooke was merely a minor fiction writer without original talent. In *John Carper,* it might be argued, he had imitated Cooper; in

The Chevalier Merlin, Scott. A careful examination of his tales, however, will leave the impression that the argument is too easy, that only in the general sense in which most novelists are imitators was Cooke an imitator of his predecessors or his contemporaries. In narrative skill, invention, and style his fiction displays merits distinctly superior to the product of one who has merely copied greater men.

This is not to say that Cooke possessed literary genius of the highest order; nor is it to imply that he was untouched by the writers of his generation or the spirit of the age in which he lived. Somehow he learned to write, doubtless in part through study of what others had done. He was too original, however, to borrow more than a principle; and of specific influence by his contemporaries or immediate predecessors, his mature fiction contains little or none. For example, Poe, whose tales Cooke strongly praised and with whom Cooke's relations were closer than with any other writer except his cousin, John Pendleton Kennedy. Yet in neither Cooke's verse nor his fiction is there anything that appears to be due to the influence of Poe, whose value to the younger man lay in commendation of his lyrics to lecture audiences and publishers rather than in provision of models for metrical or prose imitation. In fact, the positive influence of Kennedy, though not great—Cooke may have got the idea of writing about pioneer and rural Virginia from Kennedy's *Horse Shoe Robinson* and *Swallow Barn*—apparently was larger than that of Poe.

As for other writers of Cooke's generation, it has already been suggested in the discussion of his poetry that there could have been little if any influence through personal contact. The records compel a similar conclusion with regard to the prose. Cooke conversed with John Pendleton Kennedy during the latter's occasional visits to the Valley. He associated as an intimate friend and hunting companion with Kennedy's brother, Philip Pendleton Kennedy, author of the little-known, anonymous narrative, *The Blackwater Chronicle*. But it is not certain that he ever met another writer in the flesh. Probably he did meet Nathaniel Beverley Tucker, though their correspondence suggests nothing more than a literary acquaintanceship. Cooke also corresponded with, and may have been acquainted with, Benjamin Blake Minor and John R. Thompson, editors of *The Southern Literary Messenger* after the death of Thomas W. White. He corresponded briefly, in 1848, with Henry B. Hirst, editor of *The Illustrated Courier,* and invited Hirst to visit the Vineyard; but this never occurred. Finally, he corresponded with Rufus W. Griswold, but there is nothing to indicate that the two ever saw one another.

Such was the scope of Cooke's association with authors. The fact is that as a literary man Cooke led an extraordinarily isolated life, even for a Southerner in a South where, except for the Charleston group of Simms and the Richmond gentlemen who clustered around the *Messenger,* there was little that might be compared with the Cambridge-Boston school, the aging Knickerbockers, or the Philadelphia literary clans. Obviously, little in Cooke's fiction can be due to the influence of literary fellowship. And of the general influence that comes from reading one's contemporaries and evaluating their performances, there is no more than there is of the influence of Froissart in Cooke's ballads.

Actually, there is less. In temperament, Cooke was closer to the age of Froissart than to the times and scenes in which he lived; and as his talent for fiction matured, he inclined naturally to the romance of the distant past. His achievement is evidence of an original and gifted mind. For only such a mind, cut off as was his from the stimulus of its fellows, could have created a work as distinctive as *The Chevalier Merlin.*

CHAPTER VII

Last Years

RELATIVELY industrious in composition as were the last three years of his life, Cooke apparently gained little financially from the labors of his pen. On the other hand, he did not permit literature to overshadow completely the pursuits appropriate to a Virginia country gentleman. "We have a party to dine with us today," he wrote to his father in September, 1847, "and I am obliged to ride up to Millwood before company come, to catch a mason and bring him down to plaster my cistern; so I have not time to write more than a few additional words. Tell Ma I was rejoiced to receive her long and affectionate letter, and that I have not answered it because we have all been in a round of country pleasures, and I have not had the mental freedom, or the quiet, to do so in a good hearty manner. Love to her—and Mary—and yourself—from Anne and our children. I send a goodly share from myself. God bless you."[1]

The evidence for the meager reward of authorship is mainly negative, except for a passage in a letter from the *Messenger* editor, John R. Thompson, to Cooke:

1. Cooke Collection. Letter dated September 16, 1847. It also informed: "In reference to my own visit to Richmond this fall, if I go I shall have to be at the expense of refitting my dress wardrobe, as I am a little rubby at the buttons of my last costly Baltimore suit bought 18 months ago. I shall do uncommonly well without such an outlay until next spring, if I remain in the country. Besides I am slowly paying some fag ends of debts, which 50 dols. (which I should take with me for my travelling expenses) would nearly cover. After March 1st 1848 I fancy I shall be able to enlarge the horison of my enjoyments a little, and the trip may then be taken without discomfort or breach of economics."

"The best way in which I could possibly conclude this scrawling epistle would be in writing you a check for the amount of my indebtedness to you, but as I am still in the vocative case with reference to the substantive, *Pecunia*, I must continue still longer to be your debtor, and to draw on your patience instead of my banker. Whatsoever opinions I may have secured 'from all sorts of people' about The Messenger it is pretty certain I have had no 'golden' ones, so that, with thanks for your friendly forbearance hitherto, I must now close with no more 'valuable consideration' than the warmest regards. . . ."[2] There is nothing to suggest that Thompson was ever able to close with consideration more valuable than his regards.

But despite the demands of hospitality and the slightness of the returns from authorship, Cooke could look back on his thirty-third birthday to a half-decade of creditable achievement. He had written excellent poetry. He had established himself as a novelist of talent. He had made literary friends who could be useful to him. And this he had done without prejudice to his mode of living or to his pride as a Virginia gentleman.

For concerned to have the world's esteem, he had never greatly been. "I look upon these matters serenely," he had written to Thompson, "and will treat renown as Sir Thomas More advises concerning guests—welcome its coming when it cometh, hinder not with oppressive eagerness when it goeth." Furthermore, he was of the temper to look placidly upon the profile of this same renown, if, instead of stopping, it went by to take up with another. Therefore, it would not ruffle him to see Thompson win away from him the honors of Southern letters.[3] But renown—

---

2. University of Virginia Library. Copy of a letter, John R. Thompson to Philip Pendleton Cooke, dated October 17, 1848. Cooke's letter to Thompson, to which the foregoing is in answer, apparently has not been preserved.

3. F. V. N. Painter, "Philip Pendleton Cooke," *Library of Southern Literature*, III, 1063. Painter quotes from a letter no longer extant.

at least, a growing reputation—had come, and he had serenely welcomed its coming. He could reasonably look forward to a long period of satisfaction in its company.

What direction Cooke's career would have taken, had he lived, it is fair to infer from his course hitherto and from his circumstances at the time of his death. From poetry, in which branch of literature his performance had been certainly respectable, he had turned to prose, disappointed by the financial failure of *Froissart Ballads* and perhaps discouraged by the growing general indifference to that form of poetry, the ballad, which most agreed with his temperament and most fully called into play his poetic gifts. In prose, he had written several critical essays, sane, clear, illuminating—devoid, it is true, of thin-spun critical theory, and perhaps not very original, but adequate to the pages of the *Messenger;* adequate, moreover, to reveal sound technical knowledge of the craft of the teller of tales.

Then had come Cooke's experiments in fiction. Despite their blemishes—blemishes more-or-less common to the tales of Cooper, of Simms, and, in fact, of most of the fiction writers of Cooke's generation except Poe—they had displayed and had given development to certain natural gifts of high order essential to the great romantic novelist: a feeling for color, pageantry, background; a fine sense of the externally dramatic; a command of dialogue and a sharp ear for the nuances of speech; an easy, informal style—a style lean, economical, vigorous, and swift, and yet, notwithstanding these qualities which impress one in retrospect, a style always subordinated to the action or the thought to be conveyed. Such gifts pointed clearly to the field of the historical romance. And *The Chevalier Merlin,* unfinished though it is, proves that Cooke had at last found the vehicle most appropriate, in his age, for his talents.

The economic status of his family, a factor of first importance in determining the performance of a talent such as Cooke's, seemed even more assured than it had been during the early days at Vineyard. By the death of Nathaniel Burwell in November, 1849, Willianne Cooke was about to come into full possession of her ample inheritance. That, to Cooke, could not have been quite like an inheritance from a once rich and lavishly generous father; nor could it have been so satisfying as would have been a competence won by the labors of his own pen. But it meant security for his own immediate family. It meant, too, ability to aid his father should pressing need arise. And it meant the freedom from worry, and the means of relaxation through the modest diversions of a country gentleman, which were essential to the fluent expression of his creative powers.

So pleasantly circumstanced, Cooke could have followed, it would seem, only one career had he lived: the career of the novelist. Poetry would have been an avocation, in which, indeed, he might have dashed off a "Florence Vane" or a "Geoffrey Tetenoire" for the applause of table companions. Literary criticism would have been the diversion of an active mind studious to observe the methods of master romancers. Prose fiction would have been his serious business as an author.[4] And had he lived through the decade of the fifties, there might well have been a score of notable tales to add to his novelettes and *The Chevalier Merlin*. Had he survived the War Between the States, there might well have been a series of stirring historical dramas related with a sureness of touch and a sense of proportion in word

4. What is probably the last letter from Cooke to his father (one of the few extant letters to the father for the last two years of Cooke's life) contains a passage which suggests with what earnestness he practiced authorship. Mainly concerned with advice to John Esten and with affairs of the Burwell estate, it closes: "I am positively sick with writing and chewing before a hot fire. I have done a morning's work at my novel before writing this."—Cooke Collection. Letter dated November 29, 1849.

and deed not always displayed by those who did live to write about that conflict.

But such was not to be the pattern which fate had arranged for Philip Pendleton Cooke. In January, 1850, he went hunting; and to retrieve a wounded duck that had fallen into the Shenandoah, he waded into the icy river. Cold developed from the exposure. Pneumonia swiftly followed. On Sunday, January 20, 1850, Cooke died at the Vineyard.[5]

So ended in sharp circumstance the career of Philip Pendleton Cooke—gentleman, hunter, and Virginia's finest poet and romancer. It was a career too soon ended, and it may be that in moments of lingering consciousness Cooke wondered at the sharpness. Still, over against the sharpness might be set allaying recollections. He had lived the sort of life that suited his temperament. He had lived honorably. He had been, especially in the last years, greatly happy. He had found, and admirably used, literary forms well adapted to his gifts. And using those forms, he had won reputation and the esteem of those whose opinions he deemed of value. That much achieved, a gentleman might face, not too impotently, the ultimate countenance of fate.

It was, however, a career too soon ended, whatever the factors that might have helped to soften the contour of death. For though longevity scarcely could have brought

5. Information supplied by Mrs. A. B. Bevan. Practically no details regarding Cooke's death are given in the various sketches of his career. For example, Dr. W. H. Whiting, Jr., whose ancestral home is almost in sight of Vineyard, contents himself in his discussion of Cooke with this sentence: "Mr. Cooke died Jan. 20, 1850, not yet thirty-four years of age." ("Philip Pendleton Cooke," *Hampden-Sydney Magazine*, April, 1928, p. 11.) In Cooke's file in the Princeton alumni office is a newspaper clipping which relates that Cooke was "drowned in the Opequan creek near 'The Bower' in Jefferson county, late one fall while hunting." Attached is a letter from N. L. W. Pendleton, dated January 21, 1910. Pendleton doubtless was in some degree related to Cooke; but the clipping, of which he was perhaps the author, hardly deserves to be credited. Another tradition in the Valley, perhaps a sounder one, is that the practice of blood-letting hastened the course of Cooke's illness, if it did not cause his

Last Years

greater happiness than Cooke had known, or an addition to his talents, it could have brought full accomplishment. That would have added a rich chapter to the history of American literature.

---

death. Certainly the end came quickly. Mrs. Bevan possesses a letter composed shortly after the event by one of Cooke's Martinsburg cousins, Edmund Pendleton. A passage reads: "The loss of such a man—such a friend—such a relative, the pride of his kindred—under any circumstances, deeply grievous, is rendered still more so by its sudden and unexpected communication to us, and by the painful ignorance on our part of the character of the disease." The body of Cooke was buried in the churchyard cemetery of Old Chapel, near Millwood, where he occasionally worshipped with the Episcopalian gentry of the neighborhood. The branches of a willow tree spread over his grave. Carved in the marble is the form of a lyre, like that over the grave of Keats.

Bibliography

(All the materials used in Philip Pendleton Cooke: A Critical and Biographical Study are included. The first division lists Cooke's published work, arranged in order of publication. Items reprinted by *The Southern Literary Messenger* or in *Froissart Ballads, and Other Poems* are so noted.)

I. Cooke's Writings

1. VERSE

"Song of the Sioux Lovers," *The Knickerbocker Magazine*, II (July, 1833), 60.

"Autumn," *The Knickerbocker Magazine*, II (November, 1833), 368.

"The Consumptive," *The Knickerbocker Magazine*, III (February, 1834), 99-100.

"Dhu Nowas," *The Knickerbocker Magazine*, III (April, 1834), 292.

"There's a Season" (untitled), reprinted from *The Winchester* (Va.) *Republican* in *The Gazette,* Martinsburg, W. Va., January 29, 1835.

"The Creation of the Antelope," *The Southern Literary Messenger*, I (January, 1835), 216.

"A Song of the Seasons," *The Southern Literary Messenger*, I (January, 1835), 232.

"Young Rosalie Lee," *The Southern Literary Messenger*, I (March, 1835), 332. *Froissart Ballads.*

"The Last Indian," *The Southern Literary Messenger*, I (April, 1835), 402-403.

Bibliography

"Carriers' Address to the Patrons of The Winchester Republican, January 1, 1836." Printed by *The Republican*. Only known copy, printed on satin, in the possession of Mrs. A. B. Bevan, Millwood, Va.

"Lady Leonore and Her Lover," *The Southern Literary Messenger*, II (January, 1836), 109-110.

"The Huma," in the essay "A Leaf from My Scrap Book," *The Southern Literary Messenger*, II (May, 1836), 372.

"Lines," *The Southern Literary Messenger*, II (August, 1836), 557.

"The Ballad of Count Herman," in the Kennedy Memoir; first known publication in the article "An Unpublished Poem of Philip Pendleton Cooke," by W. J. Hogan, *The Educational Forum*, I (November, 1936), 81-86.

"January 1, 1838," clipping, Dr. R. P. Cooke, Lexington, Va. (Carriers' Address).

"Sonnet—To Mary," *The Southern Literary Messenger*, IV (August, 1838), 488.

"On Dreaming That I Heard a Lady Engaged in Prayer," *The Southern Literary Messenger*, IV (August, 1838), 542.

"Lines on the Sudden Death of a Very Dear Friend," *The Southern Literary Messenger*, VI (September, 1840), 675. Reprinted as "An Old Unpublished Poem. From Philip P. Cooke, of 'Vineyard,' to Lewis Burwell, 'Prospect Hill,'" *The Clarke Courier*, Berryville, Va., May, 1882. (Clipping in the possession of Dr. R. P. Cooke, Lexington, Va.)

"Earl March and His Daughter," *Burton's Gentleman's Magazine*, February, 1840, p. 92.

"Florence Vane," *Burton's Gentleman's Magazine*, March, 1840, p. 108. Reprinted in "A Letter about Florence Vane," *The Southern Literary Messenger*, XVI (June, 1850), 369-370. *Froissart Ballads*.

"Love and Care," *The Southern Literary Messenger*, VI (March, 1840), 163.

"Life in the Autumn Woods," *The Southern Literary Messenger*, IX (December, 1843), 729-730. *Froissart Ballads*.

"The Power of the Bards," *The Southern Literary Messenger*, IX (December, 1843), 744. *Froissart Ballads*.

"Emily. Proem to the 'Froissart Ballads,'" *Graham's Magazine*, XXVIII (January, 1846), 30-32. *Froissart Ballads*.
"The Mountains," *The Broadway Journal*, II (December 20, 1845). Reprinted in *The Southern Literary Messenger*, XII (May, 1846), 265-267. *Froissart Ballads*.
"The Murder of Cornstalk," *The Southern Literary Messenger*, XII (June, 1846), 337-339. *Froissart Ballads*.
"Love and Be Kind," *The Southern Literary Messenger*, XII (July, 1846), 426. *Froissart Ballads*.
"To My Daughter Lily," *Graham's Magazine*, XXIX (August, 1846), 66. *Froissart Ballads*.
"Lines," *Graham's Magazine*, XXIX (September, 1846), 143. Reprinted with title "To Edith," in *Froissart Ballads*.
"Geoffrey Tetenoire," *The Southern Literary Messenger*, XIII (March, 1847), 145-147. *Froissart Ballads*.
"The Master of Bolton," *Froissart Ballads*.
"Orthone," *Froissart Ballads*.
"Sir Peter of Bearn," *Froissart Ballads*.
"Our Lady's Dog," *Froissart Ballads*.
"Imaginary Ills," *Froissart Ballads*.
"The Famine Tower," in the article "Dante," *The Southern Literary Messenger*, XII (September, 1846), 545-554. Reprinted with the title "The Story of Ugolino," in *Froissart Ballads*.
"The Death of Arnold Winkelried," *The Southern Literary Messenger*, XIII (October, 1847), 610-611.
"Pan and Echo," *The Illustrated Monthly Courier*, I (November 1, 1848).

2. ESSAYS

(Published in *The Southern Literary Messenger;* unpublished elsewhere.)

English Poetry, Chap. I, I (April, 1835), 397-401; Chap. II, I (June, 1835), 557-565; Chap. III, II (January, 1836), 101-106.
"Leaves from My Scrap Book," II (April, 1836), 314-316.
"Leaf from My Scrap Book" (including "The Huma"), II (May, 1836), 372.
"Old Books and New Authors," XII (April, 1846), 199-203.

Bibliography

"Dante" (including "The Famine Tower"), XII (September, 1846), 545-554.
Living Novelists, Chap. I, XIII (June, 1847), 367-373; Chap. II, XIII (September, 1847), 529; Chap. III, XIII (December, 1847), 745-752.
"Edgar A. Poe," XIV (January, 1848), 34-38.
"The Feudal Armies of France and England," XIV (June, 1848), 362-365.

3. SKETCHES AND PROSE TALES

(Except where noted, published only in *The Southern Literary Messenger*.)

John Carper, the Hunter of Lost River, Chaps. I-II, XIV (February, 1848), 90-94; Chaps. III-V, XIV (March, 1848), 167-175; Chaps. VI-VII, XIV (April, 1848), 222-228.
The Two Country Houses, Chaps. I-III, XIV (May, 1848), 307-318; Chaps. IV-V, XIV (June, 1848), 349-356; Chaps. VI-VIII, XIV (July, 1848), 436-450.
The Gregories of Hackwood, Chaps. I-III, XIV (September, 1848), 537-543; Chaps. IV-VIII, XIV (October, 1848), 612-622.
"Captain Guy; or, The Unpardonable Sin," *The Illustrated Monthly Courier,* I, No. 4 (October 2, 1848).
"Joseph Jenkin's Researches into Antiquity: Erisicthon," XIV (December, 1848), 721-726.
The Crime of Andrew Blair, Chaps. I-III, XV (January, 1849), 46-54; Chaps. IV-VI, XV (February, 1849), 101-108; Chaps. VII-VIII, XV (March, 1849), 148-154.
The Chevalier Merlin, Chaps. I-III, XV (June, 1849), 326-335; Chaps. IV-VI, XV (July, 1849), 417-426; Chaps. VII-IX, XV (August, 1849), 473-481; Chaps. X-XII, XV (September, 1849), 569-576; Chaps. XIII-XV, XV (November, 1849), 641-650; Chaps. XVI-XVII, XV (December, 1849), 727-734; Chaps. XVIII-XX, XVI (January, 1850), 42-50. (Uncompleted).
"A Morning with Cagliostro. From Notes of a Conversation with Mr. Joseph Jenkins," XVI (December, 1850), 743-752.
"The Turkey-hunter in the Closet," XVII (October-November, 1851), 659-662.

Bibliography

II. Unpublished Materials

1. MANUSCRIPTS

Cooke, John Esten. A Legend of Turkey Buzzard Hollow. Cooke Collection. Duke University Library.

———. Note Books. In possession of Dr. R. P. Cooke, Lexington, Va.

———. Personal Recollections of John Esten Cooke, the Younger. In possession of Dr. R. P. Cooke, Lexington, Va.

———. Philip Pendleton Cooke. In possession of Dr. R. P. Cooke, Lexington, Va.

Cooke, Philip Pendleton. Alumni File of, Princeton University Alumni Office.

———. Manuscript Note to "Florence Vane"; Memorandum of Fruit Trees at the Vineyard. In possession of Mrs. A. B. Bevan, Millwood, Va.

———. Hunting Record for Month of October, 1845. In possession of Dr. R. P. Cooke, Lexington, Va.

Cooke, Stephen. Alumni File of, Princeton University Alumni Office.

Cooke, Willianne Burwell. "Complaint of the Old Year, 1836." In possession of Mrs. A. B. Bevan, Millwood, Va.

Kennedy, John Pendleton. Bound Volumes: Business Memoranda, Journal 1829-39; Notebooks for 1850-1851; Letters to His Wife; Letters to His Mother. Kennedy Collection. Peabody Institute, Baltimore.

Kennedy, Philip Pendleton. Memoir of Philip Pendleton Cooke. In possession of Mrs. A. B. Bevan, Millwood, Va. Referred to in text as Kennedy Memoir.

Marriage Records. Berkeley County Courthouse, Martinsburg, W. Va.

Minutes of the Faculty. Princeton University Library.

Sparhawk, Edward Vernon. Entry from His Diary, copied in Note Book of John Esten Cooke. In possession of Dr. R. P. Cooke, Lexington, Va.

Thompson, May Alcott. Philip Pendleton Cooke. Columbia University, New York, 1923. (Master's thesis).

Bibliography

Watts, Helen Lucile. The Life and Writings of Henry Beck Hirst. Columbia University, New York, 1925. (Master's thesis).

2. LETTERS OF PHILIP PENDLETON COOKE

(Published where noted. Most important manuscript collections containing letters related to Cooke are the John Esten Cooke Collection, Duke University; the John Pendleton Kennedy Collection, Peabody Institute; and the Rufus W. Griswold Collection, Boston Public Library.)

To John R. Cooke. In Cooke Collection. Duke University Library:
 1840 October 5; November 15; December 29; December 31.
 1841 February 4; March 2; September 27; December 2.
 1842 No date (early in June); September 3; October 14; November 28.
 1843 February 1; March 10; April 26; May 2; May 17; August 10.
 1844 January 8; July 6; July 10.
 1845 April 28.
 1846 March 15; August 25; December 8.
 1847 September 16.
 1848 March 17; April 13.
 1849 November 29.

To John R. Cooke:
 1832 June 5, Miss Mariah P. Duval, Charlottesville, Va.
 1840 February 14, Miss Duval; March 22, John D. Allen, Macon, Ga.
 1841 August—, Miss Anne Meade, Baltimore; November 17, Miss Duval.
 1842 Undated, Miss Duval; September 20, Miss Meade; October 20, Miss Meade.
 1843 June 21, Miss Meade; October 13, Miss Duval; November 30, Mrs. A. B. Bevan, Millwood, Va.
 1845 March, Miss Meade; March 30, Mrs. Bevan; December 5, Miss Duval.
 1847 February 4, Miss Meade.

To Mrs. John R. Cooke:
1843 November 30, Mrs. A. B. Bevan, Millwood, Va.
To Rufus W. Griswold. In Griswold Collection. Boston Public Library:
1845 October 15.
1846 November 8; November 26; December 3.
1847 January 20; February 1; February 19.
To John Pendleton Kennedy. In Kennedy Collection. Peabody Institute, Baltimore.
1845 October 3; November 15; December 1; December 19; n.d.
1846 November 8; November 23; November 27.
To Edgar Allan Poe. In Griswold Collection:
1839 September 16, published in Harrison, James A., *Life and Letters of Edgar Allan Poe,* and elsewhere; December 19.
To Nathaniel Beverley Tucker:
1835 October 25; December 23. Coleman Manuscript Collection. Tucker House, Williamsburg, Va.
1846 August 4, published in Harrison, James A., *Life and Letters of Edgar Allan Poe,* and elsewhere.
1847 March 29. Coleman Manuscript Collection. Tucker House, Williamsburg, Va.
Miscellaneous:
1835 March. To *The Southern Literary Messenger.* Published *ibid.,* I, 388.
1847 April 29. To Carey and Hart, Publishers, Philadelphia. Yale University Library.
1848 July 27. To Carey and Hart, Publishers, Philadelphia. Ford Collection. New York Public Library. May 11. To Henry B. Hirst. Cooke Collection. (Transcript).

3. LETTERS TO PHILIP PENDLETON COOKE

From John Esten Cooke:
1848 December 31. Manuscript Division, Library of Congress.
From John R. Cooke:
1845 March 30. Mrs. A. B. Bevan, Millwood, Va.
From Henry B. Hirst:
1848 June 28. Cooke Collection. (Transcript).

Bibliography

From John Pendleton Kennedy:
  1842 June 17. J. H. Whitty, Richmond, Va.
  1845 December 22. Manuscript Division, New York Public Library. (Transcript).
  1846 June 12. Manuscript Division, New York Public Library. (Transcript).
  1846 November 26. Kennedy Collection.
From Edgar Allan Poe:
  1839 September 21. Griswold Collection. Reprinted in Harrison, James A., *Life and Letters of Edgar Allan Poe,* and elsewhere.
  1846 August 4. Published in Harrison, *Life.*
From John R. Thompson:
  1848 October 17. University of Virginia Library. (Transcript).

4. ADDITIONAL LETTERS

Cooke, Catherine Esten, to John R. Cooke:
  1817 March 22. Miss Mariah P. Duval, Charlottesville, Va.
Cooke, John Esten, to Edward St. George Cooke:
  1858 June 13. Manuscript Division, Library of Congress.
Cooke, John Esten, to John R. Cooke:
  1850 July 21. Yale University Library.
Cooke, John Esten, to Rufus W. Griswold:
  1851 February 3; June 6. Griswold Collection.
  1855 May 28. Griswold Collection.
Cooke, John R., to Dr. Henry Boteler:
  1828 February 6. Cooke Collection.
  1830 August 24. Cooke Collection.
  1832 July 10. Cooke Collection.
Cooke, Maria Pendleton, to Mrs. John R. Cooke:
  1849 March 6. Miss Mariah P. Duval, Charlottesville, Va.
Duval, Mariah Pendleton, to May Alcott Thompson:
  1923 January 26; Manuscript Division, New York Public Library.
Griswold, Rufus W., to John R. Thompson:
  1850 February 19. University of Virginia Library.

Griswold, Rufus W., to John Pendleton Kennedy:
  1845 September 22. Kennedy Collection.
  1846 February 3. Kennedy Collection.
Kennedy, John Pendleton, to Rufus W. Griswold:
  1846 January 6. Griswold Collection.
  1850 March 9. Kennedy Collection.
Kennedy, John Pendleton, to Mrs. John Kennedy:
  1838 December 2. Kennedy Collection.
Kennedy, John Pendleton, to Mrs. John Pendleton Kennedy:
  1838 March 15; March 20; September 15. Kennedy Collection.
  1839 June 4. Kennedy Collection.
Kennedy, John Pendleton, to Philip Pendleton Kennedy:
  1850 March 7; September 28. Kennedy Collection.
  1851 April 19. Kennedy Collection.
Kennedy, John Pendleton, to Philip C. Pendleton:
  1835 November 30. Kennedy Collection.
  1838 December 12. Kennedy Collection.
  1839 April 18. Kennedy Collection.
Kennedy, John Pendleton, to William Gilmore Simms:
  1851 March 8; June 15. Kennedy Collection.
  1852 February 29. Kennedy Collection.
Kennedy, Philip Pendleton, to Rufus W. Griswold:
  1851 March 28. Griswold Collection.
Pendleton, Edmund, to David Holmes McGuire:
  1850 January 23. Mrs. A. B. Bevan, Millwood, Va.
Poe, Edgar Allan, to James Russell Lowell:
  1844 July 2. Harvard University Library.
Simms, William Gilmore, to John Pendleton Kennedy:
  1851 April 12. Kennedy Collection.
  1852 February 17. Kennedy Collection.
Thompson, John R., to Rufus W. Griswold:
  1851 June 28. Griswold Collection.

III. General

1. BOOKS

Aler, F. Vernon. *History of Martinsburg and Berkeley County, West Virginia.* Hagerstown, Md.: Mail Publishing Company, 1880.

Bibliography

Allen, Hervey. *Israfel, The Life and Times of Edgar Allan Poe.* New York: Doran, 1927.

Beaty, John O. *John Esten Cooke, Virginian.* New York: Columbia University Press, 1922.

Campbell, Killis. *The Mind of Poe and Other Studies.* Cambridge, Mass.: Harvard University Press, 1933.

Chaucer, Geoffrey. *The Canterbury Tales,* in *The Student's Chaucer.* Ed. by W. W. Skeat. Oxford: Oxford University Press, 1929.

Cooke, Philip Pendleton. *Froissart Ballads, and Other Poems.* Philadelphia: Carey and Hart, 1847.

Cotterill, R. S. *The Old South.* Glendale, Calif.: Arthur H. Clark Co., 1936.

Froissart, Sir John. *The Chronicles of Froissart,* tr. by Lord Berners. Ed. by W. E. Henley in *The Tudor Translations.* London: David Nutt, 1902.

Gordon, Armistead C., Jr. *Virginian Writers of Fugitive Verse.* New York: James T. White & Co., 1923.

Griswold, Rufus W. *Passages from the Correspondence and Other Papers of Rufus W. Griswold.* Ed. by W. M. Griswold. Cambridge, Mass.: Privately Published, 1898.

Gwathmey, Edward M. *John Pendleton Kennedy.* New York: Nelson, 1931.

Harrison, James A. *Life and Letters of Edgar Allan Poe.* New York: Crowell, 1903.

Hart, John S. *A Manual of American Literature.* Boston: Eldredge and Brother, 1872.

Hogg, John. *The Raven, by Edgar Allan Poe, with Literary and Historical Commentary.* London: George Redway, 1885.

Howe, Henry. *Historical Collections of Virginia.* Charleston, S. C.: William R. Babcock, 1845.

Hunter, Martha T. *A Memoir of Robert M. T. Hunter.* Washington: Neale Publishing Co., 1903.

Ingram, John H. *Edgar Allan Poe.* London, 1880.

Jackson, David K. *The Contributors and Contributions to The Southern Literary Messenger* (1834-1864). Charlottesville, Va.: Historical Publishing Co., 1936.

———. *Poe and The Southern Literary Messenger*. Richmond, Va.: Dietz, 1934.

Kercheval, Samuel. *A History of the Valley of Virginia*. Strasburg, Va.: Shenandoah Publishing House, 1925. (Reprint of the revised and enlarged edition of 1850; first edition, 1833.)

Meade, Everard Kidder. *Clarke County, 1836-1936*, with a Historical Sketch by Arthur Bowie Chrisman. Berryville, Va.: Clarke Courier Press, 1936.

Minor, Benjamin Blake. *The Southern Literary Messenger, 1834-1864*. Washington: Neale Publishing Co., 1905.

Mott, Frank Luther. *A History of American Magazines, 1741-1850*. New York: Appleton, 1930.

Norris, J. E. *History of the Lower Shenandoah Valley*. Chicago: A. Warner, 1890.

Old Chapel, Clarke County, Virginia. Berryville, Va.: Blue Ridge Press, 1906.

Parks, Edd Winfield. *Southern Poets*. New York: American Book Company, 1936.

Phillips, Mary E. *Edgar Allan Poe the Man*. Foreword by J. H. Whitty. Philadelphia: Winston, 1926.

Poe, Edgar Allan. *Complete Works*. Ed. by James A. Harrison. Virginia Edition. New York: Crowell, 1902.

———. *The Works of Edgar Allan Poe*. Ed. with an Introduction by Hervey Allen. New York: Walter J. Black, 1927.

Princeton University. Untitled Catalogue for the Academic Year 1839-40. *General Catalogue of Princeton University, 1746-1906*. Princeton, N. J.: Princeton University, 1908.

Tanner, H. S. *A New Universal Atlas*. Philadelphia: Published by the Author, 1836.

Traveller's Guide Through the Middle and Northern States and the Provinces of Canada. Saratoga Springs: G. M. Davison, 1833.

Tucker, Nathaniel Beverley. *The Partisan Leader*. Ed. with an Introduction by Carl Bridenbaugh. New York: Knopf, 1933.

Tuckerman, Henry T. *The Life of John Pendleton Kennedy*. New York: Putnam, 1871.

Wade, John Donald. *Augustus Baldwin Longstreet*. New York: Macmillan, 1924.

Woodberry, George E. *Edgar Allan Poe*. Boston: Houghton, Mifflin, 1892.

2. PERIODICALS AND GENERAL REFERENCES

Allen, John D., Communication to the Editor, *The Educational Forum*, I (May, 1937), 506. (Discusses W. J. Hogan's "An Unpublished Poem of Philip Pendleton Cooke.")

Beaty, John O., "Cooke, John Esten," *Dictionary of American Biography*. New York, 1930, pp. 385-386.

Brooke, St. George Tucker, "The Brooke Family," *Virginia Historical Magazine*, XV, 453.

"Burwell. Entries from Family Bible," *Virginia Magazine of History and Biography*, XXXI (October, 1923), 357-359.

Campbell, Killis, "The Kennedy Papers," *Sewanee Review*, XXV, 348-360.

Comment on Poe Lecture, *The Weekly Tribune*, New York, March 8, 1845.

Cook, Clarence Chatham, "The Gazelle," *The New York Mirror*, May 3, 1845.

———. "Ruth," *The New York Mirror*, May 31, 1845.

Cooke, John Esten, "Deliciae Orientis," *The Southern Literary Messenger*, XVII (March, 1851).

———. "Recollections of Philip Pendleton Cooke," *The Southern Literary Messenger*, XXVI (June, 1858), 419-432.

"Cooke, Philip Pendleton," *Cyclopaedia of American Literature*. Ed. by Evert H. and George L. Duycinck. New York: Scribner, 1856.

Correspondence from Shepherdstown, *The State*, Richmond, Va., April 27, 1881.

"The First Generation of the Pendleton Family in Virginia," *William and Mary Quarterly*, XIV, No. 4 (April, 1916), 252-257.

"*Froissart Ballads*, by Philip Pendleton Cooke," *Graham's Magazine*, XXX (May, 1847), 323-324.

"*Froissart Ballads, and Other Poems*, by Philip Pendleton Cooke," *The Literary World*, I (March 27, 1847), 173-175.

"*Froissart Ballads and Other Poems*," *The Knickerbocker Magazine*, XXIX (April, 1847), 366.

Bibliography

"From Shepherdstown, Jefferson County, Va.," *The Southern Literary Messenger*, I (February, 1835), 324. (Unsigned letter).

Griswold, Rufus W., "Philip Pendleton Cooke," *The International Magazine*, IV (October, 1851), 300-303. (Reprinted in *The Southern Literary Messenger*, XVII (October-November, 1851), 669-673.)

Hawley, Frances B., "Cook, Clarence Chatham," *Dictionary of American Biography*, New York, 1930, p. 371.

Heath, James E., "Acknowledgements to Contributors," *The Southern Literary Messenger*, I (November, 1834), 128.

Hirst, Henry B., "Philip Pendleton Cooke," *Illustrated Monthly Courier*, I (October 2, 1848).

———. "Speculations in Autography," *Illustrated Monthly Courier*, I (July 1, 1848).

Hogan, W. J., "An Unpublished Poem of Philip Pendleton Cooke," *The Educational Forum*, I (November, 1936), 81-86.

Hunt, J., Jr., "A Letter About 'Florence Vane,' " *The Daily Cincinnati Gazette*, Cincinnati, Ohio, April 13, 1850. (Reprinted in *The Southern Literary Messenger*, XVI (June, 1850), 369-370.)

Hunter, Edmund Pendleton, Notice of Partnership, *The Gazette*, Martinsburg, W. Va., May 29, 1834.

———. "The Fourth of July," *The Gazette*, Martinsburg, W. Va., July 6, 1843.

Kennedy, John Pendleton, Excerpt from an Address in Congress, *The Gazette*, Martinsburg, W. Va., August 1, 1838.

Knott, H. W. Howard, "Cooke, John Rogers," *Dictionary of American Biography*, New York, 1930, pp. 386-387.

"Law School of H. St. George Tucker in Winchester," *William and Mary College Quarterly*, X (October, 1930), 310-311.

"Letter from Patrick Henry to General Adam Stephen," *Virginia Magazine of History and Biography*, XI (October, 1903), 216-218.

Lowell, James Russell, "Our Contributors, No. XVII. Edgar Allan Poe," *Graham's Magazine*, XXVII (February, 1845), 49-53.

"The Martinsburg Academy," *The Gazette,* Martinsburg, W. Va., September 10, 1840. (Advertisement).

Metcalf, John Calvin, "Cooke, Philip Pendleton," *Dictionary of American Biography,* New York, 1930, pp. 388-389.

Morrison, M. Breckinridge, "The Poetry of the Southern United States," *The Westminster Review,* CLXXXVI (July, 1911), 61-72.

Note on Virginia Economy, *Niles' Weekly Register,* June 18, 1831. (Untitled).

"Notes on New Books," *The Daily National Intelligencer,* Washington, D. C., March 18, 1847.

Note to Poem "Love and Care," *Bentley's Miscellany,* X (1841), 462.

Obituary of John R. Cooke. *The Daily Dispatch,* Richmond, Va., December 18, 1854.

Painter, F. V. N., "Philip Pendleton Cooke," *Library of Southern Literature,* Atlanta: The Martin and Hoyt Co., 1908-13, pp. 1063-1064.

"Palmyra, In Missouri," *The Enquirer,* Richmond, Va., July 21, 1835.

Pendleton, N. L. W., "Florence Vane," Newspaper Clipping in File of Philip Pendleton Cooke, Princeton University Alumni Office.

"Philip Pendleton Cooke," *The Knickerbocker Magazine,* LXIV (November, 1864), 424-426.

Poe, Edgar Allan, "A Chapter on Autography," *Graham's Magazine,* XIX (December, 1841), 273-286.

———. Editorial Notes to Correspondents, *The Broadway Journal,* I (March 15, March 22, 1845); II (September 27, December 13, December 27, 1845).

Preble, Edward, "Cooke, John Esten," *Dictionary of American Biography,* New York, 1930, pp. 384-385.

"Resolution from the Minutes of the American Whig Society, Princeton," *The Southern Literary Messenger,* XVI (March, 1850), 192.

Review of *Barons of the Potomac and Rappahannock*, by Moncure D. Conway, *Virginia Magazine of History and Biography*, I, No. 2 (October, 1893), 217-219.

"Southern Literary Messenger, No. XI," *The Enquirer*, Richmond, Va., August 21, 1835.

"The Southern Lyre," *The Southern Illustrated News*, Richmond, Va., July 4, 1863, p. 5. (Editorial).

Spaulding, Thomas M., "Cooke, Philip St. George," *Dictionary of American Biography*, New York, 1930, p. 389.

Thompson, John R., "Editor's Table," *The Southern Literary Messenger*, XVI (February, 1850), 125. (Obituary notice of Philip Pendleton Cooke.)

———. "The Late Edgar A. Poe," *The Southern Literary Messenger*, XV (November, 1849).

Tucker, Nathaniel Beverley, "Poems, by P. Cooke," *The Southern Literary Messenger*, XIII (July, 1847), 437-441.

Whiting, W. H., Jr., "Philip Pendleton Cooke," *Hampden-Sydney Magazine*, April, 1928, pp. 9-14.

"The Wynne or Winn Family," *Virginia Magazine of History and Biography*, VI (October, 1898), 203.

Index

American Whig Society, The, resolution of, 16

Battletown, Virginia, 55
Berryville, Virginia, 55
Boteler, Alexander R., 16
Brewster, Benjamin H., sketch of Cooke, 17
Bryant, William Cullen, 27, 85 n
Burwell, William Nelson, 36
Burwell, Willianne Corbin Tayloe. *See* Cooke, Mrs. Philip Pendleton.
Byron, Lord, criticized, 24; mentioned, 85

"Captain Guy; or the Unpardonable Sin," 93
"Carrier's Address," 39 n
Charlestown, removal of Cookes to, 40
Chaucer, Geoffrey, influence of on Cooke, 85
Chevalier Merlin, The, summary of, 94, 95; Poe's opinion of, 96, 97; mentioned, 46, 47 n
Coleridge, Samuel Taylor, influence of on Cooke, 85
"Consumptive, The," 21
Cooke, Catherine Esten, 10
Cooke, Henry, 52
Cooke, John Esten (the younger), description of family life, 32-33, 35; mentioned, 10, 52, 96
Cooke, John Esten (the elder), 6, 20
Cooke, John R., character of, 6-7; children of, 7 n; financial reverses of, 40-41; mentioned, 4, 21

Cooke, Mrs. John R. (Maria Pendleton), 4, 5, 40 n, 100
Cooke, Nathaniel, 6, 20
Cooke, Philip Pendleton, self-criticism, 3, 24, 41, 74-76, 82 ff; birth and ancestry, 4-5, 10; education, 4, 8, 12, 13 ff, 18; habits, 4, 10, 30-31, 33, 41, 53, 56, 77 n; early work, 4, 11-12, 21-23, 28, 38-39; personal appearance, 7, 8, 32; love of hunting and other diversion, 10-11, 32 ff, 50, 69, 93, 100, 104; reading and tastes, 11, 17-18, 42, 45, 50-51, 54, 59, 78, 85 n, 88, 99; temperament, 15-17, 27 ff, 61, 65, 90 n, 99, 101; law preparation, 20-21; law practice in Martinsburg, 23, 39, 49, 50, 52, 53-54; literary critical opinions, 24, 27, 42-43, 45-46, 50-51, 61, 72, 76 n, 77, 82; law prospects, 26-27; view on prose, 27; domestic affections, 31, 50, 53, 65; love of nature, 35; marriage, 36; children, 36 n; finances, 39, 41, 47-49, 53-57, 63-64, 100 n, 101-102; methods of composition, 46, 58-59, 68, 70, 73, 82, 95-96, 103; travel, 48-49, 51, 100; family pride, 52, 57; gardening, 59, 65-66, 74; literary ambitions, 69-70, 80; theory of poetry, 81 ff; literary talents and style, 84 ff, 93, 97 ff, 102-104; literary friends and acquaintances, 98-99
Cooke, Mrs. Philip Pendleton (Willianne Corbin Tayloe Burwell), genealogy and marriage, 36; children, 36 n; mentioned, 32-33

Index

Cooke, Philip St. George, 6, 20, 52
Cooke, Stephen, 6
Cooke, Mrs. Stephen. *See* Esten, Catherine.
Cooper, James Fenimore, Cooke compared with, 88
"Count Herman," 21
Crime of Andrew Blair, The, summary of, 90-91; mentioned, 97

Dandridge, Mary Evelina (Mrs. R. M. T. Hunter), original of "Florence Vane," 11; genealogy, 29; Cooke's attachment to, 28-31; mentioned, 14 n, 16, 89
Dandridge, Stephen, 50
"Dante," 79, 87
"Dhu Nowas," 21
"Dream, The," 22
Dumas, Alexandre, parodied, 93; mentioned, 89

"Earl March," 47
"Edgar A. Poe," 72 ff, 87, 88
"Emily," original of, 36; published, 79, 80 n
"English Poetry," 22, 25, 28, 87
"Erisicthon," 93
Esten, Catherine (Mrs. Stephen Cooke), 6-7, 10
Esten, John, governor of Bermuda, 6

"Famine Tower, The," 79, 80 n
"Feudal Armies of France and England, The," 87-88
"Florence Vane," original of, 11; praised by Poe, 67; mentioned, 16, 30, 46-47
Froissart Ballads, reviews of, 80-81; merits of, 84; financial returns from, 83 n; mentioned, 5 n, 58-59, 69, 75 ff

"Gazelle, The," wrongly credited to Cooke, 87 n
"Geoffrey Tetenoire," 82
Glengary, family life at, 32-33; social life at, 35-36; burned, 40; mentioned, 15, 20-22
"Glider, The," 22

"Goluon," 22
Gregories of Hackwood, The, summary of, 91 ff; mentioned, 97
Griswold, Rufus W., Cooke's autobiography written for, 3-4; praise of Cooke, 4-5, 84; mentioned, 62, 68, 75 ff, 81 n, 96

Hart, John S., description of Cooke, 17
Hirst, Henry B., 99
"How Sleeps My Friend," 39 n
Hunter, R. M. T., 31
Hunter, Mrs. R. M. T. *See* Dandridge, Mary Evelina.

Irving, Washington, 27, 44
"Isabel," 22

John Carper, The Hunter of Lost River, discussed, 9, 34 n, 88

Keats, John, influence of on Cooke, 85-86
"Kemp," 22
Kennedy, John Pendleton, encouragement of Cooke, 68 ff; criticism of Poe, 72; Cooke's volume dedicated to, 75; mentioned, 3, 27, 40, 58, 76 ff, 98
Kennedy, Philip Pendleton, memoir of Cooke, 8 n, 10-11, 98-99

"Lady Leonore and Her Lover," 28
"Last Indian, The," 97
"Life in the Autumn Woods," 39, 60, 97
"Lines," 79
"Living Novelists," 87
Longfellow, Henry Wadsworth, 78
"Love and Be Kind," 79
Lowell, James Russell, Poe's comparison of with Cooke, 71

Martinsburg, Virginia, description of, 8 ff; Cooke's removal to, 50; Cooke's law practice in, 50, 53-54
Martinsburg Academy, 8
"Mary Hunter of Cotsworth." *See Two Country Houses, The.*
"Master of Bolton, The," 80 n, 83, 97
"Maurice Weterbern." *See Chevalier Merlin, The.*

Millwood, 64
Minor, Benjamin Blake, 75, 99
"Morning with Cagliostro, A," 93
"Moss Troopers, The," 22
"Mountain, The," praised by Poe, 67-68; mentioned, 10, 97
"Murder of Cornstalk, The," 79, 97

"Napoleon in Egypt," 22

"Old Books and New Authors," 79, 87
Old Chapel, Virginia, 105 n
"On Dreaming I Heard a Lady Engaged in Prayer," 39 n
"Orthone," 80 n, 82

Palmyra, Missouri, journey to, 49-50, 90
"Pan and Echo," 87
Pendleton, Edmund, 105 n
Pendleton, Maria. *See* Cooke, Mrs. John R.
Pendleton, N. L. W., 105 n
Pendleton, Philip, settles in Virginia, 5
Pendleton, Philip C., advice to Cooke, 55; mentioned, 40, 68
Poe, Edgar Allan, encourages Cooke, 41 ff; praises Cooke's critical judgment, 44, 74; publishes "Florence Vane," 67; compares Cooke to Macaulay, 67-68; compares Cooke and Lowell, 71; opinion of *The Chevalier Merlin*, 96; mentioned, 39, 47, 79, 85, 98. *See also* "Edgar A. Poe."
"Power of the Bards, The," 39, 60, 79
Princeton University, Cooke educated in, 4, 12, 13 ff

"Rosalie Lee," 23-24

Scott, Sir Walter, influence of on Cooke, 85, 89, 94
"Season of Youth, The," 22
Shelley, Percy Bysshe, 85
Simms, William Gilmore, 99
"Sir Peter of Bearn," 82
"Song of the Sioux Lover," 21, 97
Strother, David H., draws illustration for Cooke's poem, 11-12; mentioned, 8

Thompson, John R., 84, 96, 99
"To Mary," 39 n
"To My Daughter Lily," 60-62, 79
Tucker, Nathaniel Beverley, Cooke's letters to, 23 ff, 82; reviews *Froissart Ballads*, 81; mentioned, 29, 44, 75, 99
"Turkey-hunter in the Closet, The," 10, 34, 93
Two Country Houses, The ("Mary Hunter of Cotsworth"), summary of, 89 ff; mentioned, 10, 50 n, 97

"Ugolino," 79, 80 n

Vineyard, The, Cooke's removal to, 63; description of, 64; mentioned, 39, 55

White, T. W., 4 n, 23
Whiting, W. H., Jr., 104 n
Winchester, Virginia, Cooke's residence at, 10, 12
Wordsworth, William, influence of on Cooke, 85

www.ingramcontent.com/pod-product-compliance
Lightning Source LLC
Chambersburg PA
CBHW030116010526
44116CB00005B/276